"From *Daybreak* to *War Is A Lie* to *When the World Outlawed War* to a prodigious number of essays (and that's just since the '08 election) David Swanson combines the timeliest scholarship and logical elegance in a call to action: 'to learn how to enjoy working for the moral good for its own sake.'" — John Heuer, Veterans for Peace.

"One of the best ways to radicalize someone's thinking is to force the person to look at a cherished ideal in a fundamentally new way. David Swanson does that with War, an ideal cherished by too many Americans. Can the United States ever be weaned from its love affair with war — Endless War? This book provides the background for dealing with that question." — William Blum, author of *Killing Hope, and of Freeing the World to Death*.

"How many Americans know that an American peace movement in the 1920s mobilized millions of people, and eventually the U.S. government, to get the world's major powers to formally renounce war? Or that the Kellogg-Briand Pact is still on the books making our current leaders guilty of the same crime that we hung people for at Nuremberg? It's time for a little education! David Swanson has written a wonderfully well-documented history of a time when Americans discovered their own power to organize and impact their government on the most vital issue facing the world, then and now: the abolition of war." — Nicolas Davies, author of *Blood On Our Hands: the American Invasion and Destruction of Iraq*.

"Polls show a large majority of U.S. citizens oppose current U.S. wars, but many Americans' reluctance to engage in antiwar activism is in part due to their sense of impotence at having any impact on their own government. This book tells the story of how the highly energized Peace Movement in the 1920s, supported by an overwhelming majority of U.S. citizens from every level of society, was able to push politicians into something quite remarkable — the Kellogg-Briand Pact and the renunciation of war as an instrument of national policy. The 1920s War Outlawry movement was so popular that most politicians could not afford to oppose it. If any one piece of American history can re-energize the American people to again push their politicians, then this book can do it." — Bruce E. Levine, author of *Get Up, Stand Up: Uniting Populists, Energizing the Defeated, and Battling the Corporate Elite.*

"'Ahhh, peace, that would be so nice,' an Afghan grandmother whispered after recounting how 30 years of war had devastated her family. The world community has failed her miserably, as it has failed so many millions from the Congo to Iraq to Sri Lanka. But David Swanson's book gives us a glimpse of another possible reality, a world that says no to war. By recounting the heroic efforts of a generation in the 1920s that actually did pass a treaty banning war, Swanson invites us to dream, to scheme and most important, to take action." — Medea Benjamin, cofounder of CODEPINK.

"David Swanson is on a mission to end war. In his latest book he brings to life an important story about a time when a national peace movement raged across our nation. The media covered this movement, and members of Congress were active participants. Through this movement a treaty was signed that outlawed war. Sadly today few know about this significant moment in our history, but Swanson's book will help change that." — Bruce K. Gagnon, Coordinator, Global Network Against Weapons & Nuclear Power in Space.

When the World Outlawed War

by David Swanson

Charlottesville, VA
First edition—2011

Also by David Swanson
WAR IS A LIE (2010)
DAYBREAK: UNDOING THE IMPERIAL PRESIDENCY
AND FORMING A MORE PERFECT UNION (2009)
THE 35 ARTICLES OF IMPEACHMENT (Introduction, 2008)

• • •

Swanson, David, 1969 Dec. 1-

When the World Outlawed War

Book design by David Swanson

Printed in the USA

First Edition / November 2011

ISBN: 978-0-9830830-9-2

davidswanson.org

What We've Forgotten

There are actions we widely believe are and should be illegal: slavery, rape, genocide. War is no longer on the list. It has become a well-kept secret that war is illegal, and a minority view that it should be illegal. I believe we have something to learn from an earlier period in our history, a period in which a law was created that made war illegal for the first time, a law that has been forgotten but is still on the books.

In 1927-1928 a hot-tempered Republican from Minnesota named Frank who privately cursed pacifists managed to persuade nearly every country on earth to ban war. He had been moved to do so, against his will, by a global demand for peace and a U.S. partnership with France created through illegal diplomacy by peace activists. The driving force in achieving this historic breakthrough was a remarkably unified, strategic, and relentless U.S. peace movement with its strongest support in the Midwest; its strongest leaders professors, lawyers, and university presidents; its voices in Washington, D.C., those of Republican senators from Idaho and Kansas; its views welcomed and promoted by newspapers, churches, and women's groups all over the country; and its determination unaltered by a decade of defeats and divisions.

The movement depended in large part on the new political power of female voters. The effort might have failed had Charles

Lindbergh not flown an airplane across an ocean, or Henry Cabot Lodge not died, or had other efforts toward peace and disarmament not been dismal failures. But public pressure made this step, or something like it, almost inevitable. And when it succeeded — although the outlawing of war was never fully implemented in accordance with the plans of its visionaries — much of the world believed war had been made illegal. Wars were, in fact, halted and prevented. And when, nonetheless, wars continued and a second world war engulfed the globe, that catastrophe was followed by the trials of men accused of the brand new crime of making war, as well as by global adoption of the United Nations Charter, a document owing much to its prewar predecessor while still falling short of the ideals of what in the 1920s was called the Outlawry movement.

"Last night I had the strangest dream I'd ever dreamed before," wrote Ed McCurdy in 1950 in what became a popular folk song. "I dreamed the world had all agreed to put an end to war. I dreamed I saw a mighty room, and the room was filled with men. And the paper they were signing said they'd never fight again." But that scene had already happened in reality on August 27, 1928, in Paris, France. The treaty that was signed that day, the Kellogg-Briand Pact, was subsequently ratified by the United States Senate in a vote of 85 to 1 and remains on the books (and on the U.S. State Department's website) to this day as part of what Article VI of the U.S. Constitution calls "the supreme Law of the Land."

Frank Kellogg, the U.S. Secretary of State who made this treaty happen, was awarded a Nobel Peace Prize and saw his public reputation soar — so much so that the United States named a ship after him, one of the "Liberty ships" that carried war supplies to Europe during World War II. Kellogg was dead at the time. So, many believed, were prospects for world peace. But the Kellogg-Briand Pact and its renunciation of war as an instrument of national policy is something we might want to revive. This treaty gathered the adherence of the world's nations swiftly and publicly, driven by fervent public demand. We might think about how public opinion of that sort might be created anew, what insights it possessed that have yet to be realized, and what systems of communication, education, and elections would allow the public again to influence government policy, as the ongoing campaign to eliminate war — understood by its originators to be an undertaking of generations — continues to develop.

We might begin by remembering what the Kellogg-Briand Pact is and where it came from. Perhaps, in between celebrating Veterans Day, Memorial Day, Yellow Ribbon Day, Patriots Day, Independence Day, Flag Day, Pearl Harbor Remembrance Day, and the Iraq-Afghanistan Wars Day legislated by Congress in 2011, not to mention the militaristic festival that bombards us every September 11th, we could squeeze in a day marking a step toward peace. I propose we do so every August 27th. Perhaps a national focus for Kellogg-Briand Day might be on an event in the National Cathedral in Washington, D.C., (if it safely reopens following the recent earthquake) where the inscription below the Kellogg Window gives Kellogg, who is buried there, credit for having "sought equity and peace among the nations of the world." Other days could be developed into peace celebrations as well, including the International Day of Peace on September 21st, Martin Luther King Jr. Day every third Monday in January, and Mothers Day on the second Sunday in May.

We would be celebrating a step toward peace, not its achievement. We celebrate steps taken toward establishing civil rights, despite that remaining a work in progress. By marking partial achievements we help build the momentum that will achieve more. We also, of course, respect and celebrate the ancient establishment of laws banning murder and theft, although murder and theft are still with us. The earliest laws making war into a crime, something it had not been before, are just as significant and will long be remembered if the movement for the Outlawry of war succeeds. If it does not, and if the nuclear proliferation, economic exploitation, and environmental degradation that come with our wars continue, then before long there may be nobody remembering anything at all.

Another way to revive a treaty that in fact remains law would, of course, be to begin complying with it. When lawyers, politicians, and judges want to bestow human rights on corporations, they do so largely on the basis of a court reporter's note added to, but not actually part of, a Supreme Court ruling from over a century back. When the Department of Justice wants to "legalize" torture or, for that matter, war, it reaches back to a twisted reading of one of the Federalist Papers or a court decision from some long forgotten era. If anyone in power today favored peace, there would be every justification for recalling and making use of the Kellogg-Briand Pact. It is actually law. And it is far more recent law than the U.S.

Constitution itself, which our elected officials still claim, mostly unconvincingly, to support. The Pact, excluding formalities and procedural matters, reads in full,

> The High Contracting Parties solemnly [sic] declare in the names of their respective peoples that they condemn recourse to war for the solution of international controversies, and renounce it, as an instrument of national policy in their relations with one another.

> The High Contracting Parties agree that the settlement or solution of all disputes or conflicts of whatever nature or of whatever origin they may be, which may arise among them, shall never be sought except by pacific means.

The French Foreign Minister Aristide Briand, whose initiative had led to the Pact and whose previous work for peace had already earned him a Nobel Peace Prize, remarked at the signing ceremony,

> For the first time, on a scale as absolute as it is vast, a treaty has been truly devoted to the very establishment of peace, and has laid down laws that are new and free from all political considerations. Such a treaty means a beginning and not an end. . . . [S]elfish and willful war which has been regarded from of old as springing from divine right, and has remained in international ethics as an attribute of sovereignty, has been at last deprived by law of what constituted its most serious danger, its legitimacy. For the

future, branded with illegality, it is by mutual accord truly and regularly outlawed so that a culprit must incur the unconditional condemnation and probably the hostility of all his co-signatories.

THE WAR TO END WAR

The peace movement that made the Kellogg-Briand Pact happen, just like the militarism against which it competed, was given a huge boost by World War I — by the scale of that war and its impact on civilians, but also by the rhetoric through which the United States had been brought into the war in 1917. In his 1952 account of this period *Peace in Their Time: The Origins of the Kellogg-Briand Pact*, Robert Ferrell noted the incredible financial and human cost of the war:

> *For years afterward, until the second World War made such older calculations wearisome, publicists impressed upon the popular mind the number of houses or libraries or colleges or hospitals which could have been purchased for the cost of the World War. The human waste was incalculable. The fighting had killed ten million men outright — one life for every ten seconds of the war's duration. No figures could tell the cost in stunted and deformed bodies and in dilapidated minds.*

And here's Thomas Hall Shastid in his 1927 book *Give the People Their Own War Power*, which argued for requiring a public referendum before launching any war:

> *[O]n November 11, 1918, there ended the most unnecessary, the most financially exhausting, and the most terribly fatal of*

all the wars that the world has ever known. Twenty millions
of men and women, in that war, were killed outright, or
died later from wounds. The Spanish influenza, admittedly
caused by the War and nothing else, killed, in various lands,
one hundred million persons more.

According to U.S. Socialist Victor Berger, all the United States had gained from participation in World War I was the flu and prohibition. It was not an uncommon view. Millions of Americans who had supported World War I came, during the years following its completion on November 11, 1918, to reject the idea that anything could ever be gained through warfare. Sherwood Eddy, who coauthored *The Abolition of War* in 1924, wrote that he had been an early and enthusiastic supporter of U.S. entry into World War I and had abhorred pacifism. He had viewed the war as a religious crusade and had been reassured by the fact that the United States entered the war on a Good Friday. At the war front, as the battles raged, Eddy writes, "we told the soldiers that if they would win we would give them a new world."

Eddy seems, in a typical manner, to have come to believe his own propaganda and to have resolved to make good on the promise. "But I can remember," he writes, "that even during the war I began to be troubled by grave doubts and misgivings of conscience." It took him 10 years to arrive at the position of complete Outlawry, that is to say, of wanting to legally outlaw all war. By 1924 Eddy believed that the campaign for Outlawry amounted, for him, to a noble and glorious cause worthy of sacrifice, or what U.S. philosopher William James had called "the moral equivalent of war." Eddy now argued that war was "unchristian." Many came to share that view who a decade earlier had believed Christianity required war. A major factor in this shift was direct experience with the hell of modern warfare, an experience captured for us by the British poet Wilfred Owen in these famous lines:

> *If in some smothering dreams you too could pace*
> *Behind the wagon that we flung him in,*
> *And watch the white eyes writhing in his face,*
> *His hanging face, like a devil's sick of sin;*
> *If you could hear, at every jolt, the blood*
> *Come gargling from the froth-corrupted lungs,*
> *Obscene as cancer, bitter as the cud*
> *Of vile, incurable sores on innocent tongues,*
> *My friend, you would not tell with such high zest*
> *To children ardent for some desperate glory,*
> *The old Lie; Dulce et Decorum est*
> *Pro patria mori.*

The propaganda machinery invented by President Woodrow Wilson and his Committee on Public Information had drawn Americans into the war with exaggerated and fictional tales of German atrocities in Belgium, posters depicting Jesus Christ in khaki sighting down a gun barrel, and promises of selfless devotion to making the world safe for democracy. The extent of the casualties was hidden from the public as much as possible during the course of the war, but by the time it was over many had learned something of war's reality. And many had come to resent the manipulation of noble emotions that had pulled an independent nation into overseas barbarity.

Eddy resented the World War I propaganda and saw war as requiring propaganda: "We cannot successfully run a modern war if we tell the truth, the whole truth, and nothing but the truth. We must always carefully repress two sets of facts: all generous statements about the foe and all unfavorable reports about ourselves and 'our glorious Allies.'"

However, the propaganda that motivated the fighting was not immediately erased from people's minds. A war to end wars and make the world safe for democracy cannot end without some lingering demand for peace and justice, or at least for something more valuable than the flu and prohibition. Even those rejecting the idea that the war could in any way help advance the cause of peace aligned with all those wanting to avoid all future wars — a group that probably encompassed most of the U.S. population.

Some of the blame for the start of the World War was place on secretly made treaties and alliances. President Wilson backed the ideal of public treaties, if not necessarily publicly negotiated treaties. He made this the first of his famous 14 points in his January 8, 1918, speech to Congress:

Open covenants of peace must be arrived at, after which there will surely be no private international action or rulings of any kind, but diplomacy shall proceed always frankly and in the public view.

Wilson had come to see popular opinion as something to use, rather than avoid. But he had learned to manipulate it with skillful propaganda, as through his successful sales pitch for U.S. entry into the war in 1917. Nonetheless, it appeared true then, and it appears true now, that greater dangers lie in government secrecy than in governance controlled by public opinion.

A MOVEMENT
BUT NO PEACE

Following the war, many in the United States, disillusioned with the war's promises, came to distrust European peace efforts, since European entanglements had created the war. When the Treaty of Versailles, on June 28, 1919, imposed a cruel victors' justice on Germany, Wilson was seen as having betrayed his word and the armistice agreement. When Wilson promised that the League of Nations would right all the wrongs of that treaty, many were skeptical, particularly as the League bore some resemblance to the sort of alliances that had produced the World War in the first place.

Both jingoistic isolationists and internationalist peace activists with a vision of Outlawry that shunned the use of force even to punish war rejected the League, as did the United States Senate, dealing a major blow to those peace advocates who believed the League was not only advantageous but also the reward due after so much suffering in the war. Efforts to bring the United States in as a member of the World Court failed as well. A Naval Disarmament Conference in Washington in 1921-1922 did perhaps more harm than good. And in 1923 and 1924 respectively, the members of the League of Nations in Europe failed to ratify a Draft Pact for Mutual Assistance and an agreement called the Geneva Protocol for the Pacific Settlement of International Disputes, both of which had adopted some of the language of the U.S. Outlawry movement to somewhat different purposes.

Remarkably, these set-backs did not halt the momentum of the peace movement in the United States or around the world. The institutional funding and structure of the peace movement was enough to make any early twenty-first century peace activist drool with envy, as was the openness of the mass media of the day, namely newspapers, to promoting peace. Leading intellectuals, politicians, robber barons, and other public figures poured their resources into the cause. A defeat or two, or 10, might discourage some individuals, but it was not about to derail the movement. Neither was political partisanship, as peace groups pressured Democrats and Republicans alike, and both responded. It was during the relatively peaceful Republican interlude of Harding, Coolidge, and Hoover, in between the extreme Democratic war making of Wilson and Roosevelt, that the peace movement reached its height.

After the turn of century, the World Peace Foundation and the Carnegie Endowment for International Peace had been created, adding energy to existing peace societies in the United States and developing a new concept: pacifism. Andrew Carnegie sought to "hasten the abolition of international war, the foulest blot upon our civilization." In 1913 he funded a Peace Palace at The Hague as a home for the Permanent Court of Arbitration, a court of which the United States was and still is a member, but a court that provided dispute resolution services as opposed to ruling on the violation of laws.

Early in the 20th century Congressman Richard Barthold proposed a Union of Nations with decisions not to be enforced militarily. In 1910, the World Peace Foundation opposed the whole system of war. Anna Eckstein promoted a petition for a proposal at the Third Hague Conference to pledge the use of only peaceful means, to be enforced by economic boycott and a court of arbitration. The idea that you could not end war by lining up allies who would punish an aggressor through the use of . . . war was American wisdom, less shared in Europe.

Yet, in 1910 Theodore Roosevelt in his Nobel Peace Prize acceptance speech spoke for those who thought war should indeed be used to enforce peace. Roosevelt himself, of course, used the U.S. military for far different purposes, but his Nobel speech exemplified the thinking that would later support the League of Nations, and later still the United Nations:

> [I]t would be a masterstroke if those great powers honestly bent on peace would form a League of Peace, not only to keep the peace among themselves, but to prevent, by force if necessary, its being broken by others.

Then, in 1914, war came to Europe, and U.S. peace groups opposed it. A new National Peace Federation was created. Jane Addams and Carrie Chapman Catt created the Woman's Peace Party. A 1915 convention in Philadelphia created a League to Enforce Peace. Henry Ford chartered a ship and took peace delegates to Europe, President Wilson having rejected Ford's offer to include official government delegates.

Wilson was reelected in 1916 on peace slogans, including "He kept us out of war." Wilson admitted in 1916 that "force will not accomplish anything that is permanent," but in 1917 he demanded "force to the utmost, force without stint or limit, the righteous and triumphant force that shall make right the law of the world." Such is the fate of campaign promises. But that language ("make right the law of the world") would come back to bite the forces of militarism, just as Wilson's democratic rhetoric was turned against him on the banners of the suffragettes protesting at the White House, enduring abuse and prison, and going on hunger strikes until women obtained the right to vote.

As Wilson talked up peace as the official reason for going to war, countless souls took him extremely seriously. "It is no exaggeration to say that where there had been relatively few peace schemes before the World War," writes Ferrell, "there now were hundreds and even thousands" in Europe and the United States. The decade following the war was a decade of searching for peace: "Peace echoed through so many sermons, speeches, and state papers that it drove itself into the consciousness of everyone. Never in world history was peace so great a desideratum, so much talked about, looked toward, and planned for, as in the decade after the 1918 Armistice."

This was the case in Europe perhaps even more than in the United States. European trade unions were pacifist and were working to recover the prewar idea of a general strike to prevent any movement towards war. Many political parties in Europe were strongly in favor of working to ensure peace. European peace organizations themselves were smaller and less influential than their U.S. counterparts, but they were more unified in their agenda. They favored both disarmament and the League of Nations, as well as other treaties, alliances, and arbitration agreements.

In a September 1928 article in the *American Review of Reviews* Frank Simonds described how U.S. and European peace advocates had approached the problem from opposite directions. Americans viewed peace as the norm and as consisting of the absence of war, he wrote. But Europeans, dealing with constant threats, provocations, grievances, and divisions, believed peace to require an elaborate system of checks on hostilities and means of resolving disputes. The United States imagined the world at peace and sought to preserve it. Europeans strove to build a peace they did not know, with a keen awareness that they could never possibly solve every dispute to everyone's satisfaction.

Many U.S. peace groups, it should be said however, inclined toward the European perspective, while others did not. The United States had a larger peace movement than Europe did, but a more deeply divided one. Sincere advocates of peace came down on both sides of the questions of joining the League of Nations and the World Court. Nor did they all see eye to eye on disarmament. If something could be found that would unite the entire U.S. peace movement, the U.S. government of the day was sufficiently representative of the public will that whatever that measure was, it was bound to be enacted.

The Carnegie Endowment had profited from the war through U.S. Steel Corporation bonds. The Endowment's president,

Dr. Nicholas Murray Butler, and its director of the Division of Economics and History, Professor James Thomson Shotwell, would play significant roles in the creation of the Kellogg-Briand Pact, after having advocated unsuccessfully for U.S. membership in the League of Nations. Shotwell had a $600,000 annual budget, or about $6.8 million in today's terms. The World Peace Foundation, a U.S. organization, had a $1 million endowment (or $11.3 million in today's terms) and, like the Carnegie Endowment, supported the League and the Court. Other major groups included the Foreign Policy Association, the League of Nations Non-Partisan Association, the Woodrow Wilson Foundation, the Church Peace Union and the World Alliance for International Friendship, as well as the Federal Council of Churches of Christ and its Commission on International Justice and Goodwill.

Another U.S. group, the American Foundation, administered the Bok Peace Plan Award, which in 1922 offered $100,000 for a winning five thousand-word peace plan. Among 22,165 plans submitted was one from William Jennings Bryan (who had resigned as Secretary of State when President Wilson had lied about the contents of the *Lusitania* in order to build up war support) and one from Franklin Delano Roosevelt, although the winner was Charles H. Levermore.

More radical peace groups, often with less funding, in some cases supported the League and the Court, but they pushed for disarmament and opposed militarism, including U.S. imperialism in Central and South America, more consistently. Ferrell described the growth of this movement:

After the 1918 Armistice scores of new peace groups mushroomed into existence. The usual procedure was first to choose an impressive name and to select appropriate stationery (ordinarily a propagandistic, name-studded letterhead). There then began a frenzied round of fund-raising, conventioning, writing to congressmen. It was truly remarkable the amount of activity these crusading peace groups could generate.

Among these organizations were the American Friends Service Committee (100,000 members), American Goodwill Association (5,000), American School Citizenship League, Arbitration Crusade, Association for Peace Education, Association to Abolish War (400), Catholic Association for International Peace, Committee on Militarism in Education, Corda Fratres Association of Cosmopolitan Clubs (1,000), Fellowship for a Christian Social Order (2,500), Fellowship of Reconciliation (4,500), Fellowship of Youth for Peace, Friends General Conference (20,000), Intercollegiate Peace Association, National Committee on the Cause and Cure of War, National Council for Prevention of War, Parliament of Peace and Universal Brotherhood, Peace Association of Friends in America (90,000), Peace Heroes Memorial Society, School World Friendship League, Society to Eliminate Economic Causes of War (150), War Resisters League (400), War Resisters International (United States Committee), Women's International League for Peace and Freedom (6,000), Women's Peace Society (2,000), Women's Peace Union of the Western Hemisphere, World Peace Association, and World Peace Mission (58), and many others.

As the names of the groups above suggest, in the 1920s women, now with the right to vote, were a major part of the antiwar movement. The American branch of the Women's International League for Peace and Freedom distributed stickers to place on income tax forms reading "That part of this income tax which is levied for preparation for War is paid only under Protest and Duress." A split in the women's peace movement led Carrie Chapman Catt to establish the National Committee on the Cause and Cure of War, which would be instrumental in pressuring senators when it came time for ratification of the Kellogg-Briand Pact.

The National Council for Prevention of War, according to Ferrell, "during the twenties laid down a barrage of peace propaganda the like of which has seldom been seen in the United States." With a budget of $113,000 in 1927 it sent out 430,000 pieces of literature. No one had thought to invent email yet, so "literature" meant hard copy pamphlets, and they tended to be read rather than deleted or sent into a spam folder.

THE OUTLAWRY OF WAR

One organization which happens to have far outstripped that volume of literature distribution deserves particular attention, although it was largely a front for a single individual and largely funded out of his own pocket. The American Committee for the Outlawry of War was the creation of Salmon Oliver Levinson. Its agenda originally attracted those advocates of peace who opposed U.S. entry into the League of Nations and international alliances. But its agenda of outlawing war eventually attracted the support of the entire peace movement when the Kellogg-Briand Pact became the unifying focus that had been missing.

William James' influence could be seen in Levinson's thinking. Levinson also collaborated closely with the philosopher John Dewey, whom James had greatly influenced, as well as with Charles Clayton Morrison, editor of *The Christian Century*, and with Senator William Borah of Idaho, who would become Chair of the Committee on Foreign Relations just when he was needed there. Dewey had supported World War I and been criticized for it by Randolphe Bourne and Jane Addams, among others. Addams would also work with Levinson on Outlawry; they were both based in Chicago. It was the experience of World War I that brought Dewey around. Following the war, Dewey promoted peace education in schools and publicly lobbied for Outlawry. Dewey wrote this of Levinson:

There was stimulus — indeed, there was a kind of inspiration
— in coming in contact with his abounding energy, which
surpassed that of any single person I have ever known.

John Chalmers Vinson, in his 1957 book, *William E. Borah and the Outlawry of War*, refers to Levinson repeatedly as "the ubiquitous Levinson." Levinson's mission was to make war illegal. And under the influence of Borah and others he came to believe that the effective outlawing of war would require outlawing all war, not only without distinction between aggressive and defensive war, but also without distinction between aggressive war and war sanctioned by an international league as punishment for an aggressor nation. Levinson wrote,

Suppose this same distinction had been urged when the institution of duelling [sic] was outlawed. . . . Suppose it had then been urged that only 'aggressive duelling' should be outlawed and that 'defensive duelling' be left intact. . . . Such a suggestion relative to duelling would have been silly, but the analogy is perfectly sound. What we did was to outlaw the institution of duelling, a method theretofore recognized by law for the settlement of disputes of so-called honor.

I've lifted this quote from John E. Stoner's 1943 account, *S. O. Levinson and the Pact of Paris: A Study in the Techniques of Influence*, a book looking back at the lessons of the 1920s peace movement even as world war raged again. Quincy Wright claims in the introduction that "it is safe to say that if Levinson had not

moved the isolationist Middle West and the isolationist Senator
Borah to support the Pact, it would not have been achieved."

Levinson wanted everyone to recognize war as an institution,
as a tool that had been given acceptability and respectability as a
means of settling disputes. He wanted international disputes to be
settled in a court of law, and the institution of war to be rejected
just as slavery had been.

Levinson understood this as leaving in place the right to self-
defense but eliminating the need for the very concept of war.
National self-defense would be the equivalent of killing an
assailant in personal self-defense. Such personal self-defense,
he noted, was no longer called "duelling." But Levinson did not
envision killing a war-making nation. Rather he proposed five
responses to the launching of an attack: the appeal to good faith,
the pressure of public opinion, the nonrecognition of gains, the
use of force to punish individual warmakers, and the use of any
means including force to halt the attack.

Levinson would eventually urge the nations signing the Kellogg-
Briand Pact (also known as the Pact of Paris) to incorporate the
following into their criminal codes: "Any person, or persons, who
shall advocate orally or in writing, or cause the publication of
any printed matter which shall advocate the use of war between
nations, in violation of the terms of the Pact of Paris, with the
intent of causing war between or among nations , shall be guilty of
a felony and upon conviction thereof shall be imprisoned not less
than _____ years." This idea can be found in the International
Covenant on Civil and Political Rights of 1966, which states: "Any

propaganda for war shall be prohibited by law." It was an idea that also influenced the Nuremberg prosecutions. It may be an idea worthy of revival and realization.

Kirby Page, another Outlawrist, in *The Abolition of War* (1924) distinguished war from "police force," meaning law enforcement by domestic police. Police force, he wrote, involves a neutral third party bringing a suspect to a court for application of the rule of law, while, in contrast, a war is judge, jury, and executioner all in one and corrupted by the passion of violence. In addition, police go after only suspected criminals, whereas a war goes after a criminal and his wife and kids and neighbors, setting in motion a process that will also likely kill family members and friends of the war makers.

In 1925 Page published *An American Peace Policy* in which he argued for the world's interdependence, the League, the World Court, and Outlawry. In arguing against the use of force to sanction a nation for its use of force, Page pointed to the failure of such a proposal in James Madison's original Virginia Plan. The U.S. Constitution does not, in fact, sanction the Union to employ force against a state (although it in fact did so against several in the Civil War). Page quotes James Brown Scott on James Madison thus:

> *The more he reflected on the use of force, the more he doubted the practicability, the justice and the efficacy of it when applied to people collectively, and not individually. A union of the States containing such an ingredient seemed to*

provide for its own destruction. The use of force against a State, would seem more like a declaration of war, than an infliction of punishment, and would probably be considered by the party attacked as a dissolution of all previous compacts by which it might be bound.

Salmon Oliver Levinson

S.O. LEVINSON
AND THE LAW

Levinson came out of the Yale class of 1888, as did Henry Stimson who was Secretary of War under Presidents William Howard Taft and Franklin Delano Roosevelt, and who followed Kellogg as Secretary of State under President Herbert Hoover. Stimson is a good example of a political figure who was moved toward peace by the climate and pressure of the times but who was also ready to distort doctrines of peace into justifications for war at the earliest shift in the cultural climate.

After Yale, Levinson went to work as a lawyer in Chicago. He believed reasonable lawyers could prevent trials. He later believed reasonable nations could prevent wars. Levinson became a skilled negotiator, a wealthy man, and the acquaintance of many wealthy and powerful people. He gave to all kinds of charities, including the peace movement.

When World War I started, Levinson organized influential people to present a peace plan to the German government. After the sinking of the *Lusitania*, Levinson — possibly ignorant of the *Lusitania*'s contents — asked Germany to "disavow" "war itself." Levinson, of course, met with no success in his efforts to halt World War I. Yet this did not seem to discourage him in the least. It is unlikely that World War II or Korea or Vietnam or the

Global War on (or is it of?) Terror would have discouraged him either. Discouragement is something we impose on ourselves, and Levinson was not inclined in that direction.

Levinson began to see the central problem as war's legality. He wrote on August 25, 1917: "War as an institution to 'settle disputes' and establish 'justice among nations' is the most barbarous and indefensible thing in civilization. . . . The real disease of the world is the legality and availability of war . . . . [W]e should have, not as now, laws of war, but laws against war; there are no laws of murdering or of poisoning, but laws against them." Others had had a similar idea before, including slavery abolitionist Charles Sumner, who called both slavery and war "institutions," but no one had ever made the idea widely known or built a campaign to realize its goals.

Emerich de Vattel (1714 - 1767) is considered a father of modern international law. He expressed the common view of his age when he wrote, "The first rule . . . is that regular war, as to its effects, is to be accounted just on both sides." In the Lieber Code of 1863, President Abraham Lincoln's guidance for the Union Army, particular atrocities were illegal but war itself was simply neutral. At Versailles, following World War I, a commission was created on the Responsibilities of the Authors of the War and on Enforcement of Penalties. A subcommission recommended prosecutions for atrocities. Another unanimously recommended against prosecutions for "acts which provoked the war." War making was not a crime.

Early in the winter of 1917 Levinson showed a draft plan to outlaw war to John Dewey, who very much approved. Levinson published an article in *The New Republic* on March 9, 1918, in which he wrote of outlawing war. Levinson, in his early writings, quoted William James' 1906 essay "The Moral Equivalent of War" which had included the line "I look forward to a future when acts of war shall be formally outlawed as between civilized people." At first Levinson favored the League of Nations and an international court using force to impose its decisions, but he came to believe such "force" was just a euphemism for war, and that war could not be ended through war.

In June of 1918 Levinson was pleased to see Prime Minister of the United Kingdom David Lloyd George speak of "making sure that war shall henceforth be treated as a crime punishable by the law of nations." Levinson at that time backed a strong League of Nations. He pitched both Outlawry and the League to peace groups including the League of Free Nations Association and the League to Enforce Peace. He organized mass meetings and other efforts, working with Jane Addams among others.

Levinson's thinking, and consequently his political agenda, evolved during the decade of the search for peace. Charles Clayton Morrison's book, *The Outlawry of War*, published with the close guidance of and dedicated to Levinson, crystallized the Outlawrists' views in 1927. Dewey wrote the Foreword, in which he argued that Outlawry would allow internationalism without political entanglement with Europe, would end the divide between individual conscience and the rule of law (a divide created by the legal status of an enterprise of mass killing), and would complete a process from barbarism to civility that had already put an end to private blood feuds and dueling. Dewey suggested that the legal status of war allowed the threat of war to facilitate the economic exploitation of weaker countries. Dewey, who was early to recognize the impact on world affairs of the combination of "the checkbook and the cruise missile" (the title of a 2004 book by Arundhati Roy), envisioned a truly new world that would be produced by banning war and eliminating the threat of it.

LEGISLATING MORALITY

Morrison's book argues for Outlawry and against alliances. U.S. Secretaries of State Elihu Root (in office 1905-1909) and William Jennings Bryan (1913-1915) had negotiated bilateral treaties of arbitration and nonaggression with various nations. Such treaties became very popular, as the nations of the world created at least 130 of them between November 11, 1918, and November 11, 1928, the bulk of them in the final four years of that period. A 1931 book by Max Habicht called *Post-War Treaties for the Pacific Settlement of International Disputes* reprints all of these treaties.

But many in the United States were averse to the sort of alliances created, for example, in 1925 in Locarno, Switzerland. Under these agreements, if Germany were to attack France, then England and Italy would have to attack Germany, whereas if France were to attack Germany, then England and Italy would have to attack France. Aristide Briand made a name for himself as a peace negotiator in Locarno, but the Outlawrists' criticism of such arrangements as sheer madness looks wiser through the lens of later history. Another such alliance is of course the North Atlantic Treaty Organization (NATO) to which the United States would become party in 1949. Another half dozen such "collective defense arrangements" would be joined by the United States during the 1950s.

The Geneva Protocol of 1924 collapsed when Britain rejected it.

Lloyd George called it the opposite of a plan to avoid war. It was, he said, "a plan for making war compulsory." Morrison agreed that uniting forces against an aggressor was a way to strengthen, not eliminate, the institution of war.

So, what was the Outlawrists' alternative? World government might work, Morrison wrote, but even if it were truly desirable, it was undoubtedly very far off in the future. Preferable, in the relatively near term, wrote Morrison, would be a world court. This would be a court of law, with the laws written down, known, and agreed to. Rather than alliances and unpredictable adjudications, the Outlawrists favored the rule of the written word.

The most popular criticism of Outlawry was that it intended to simply wish war away by banning it. The most popular criticism of international alliances was that they would create wars to end wars. While NATO and even the United Nations have indeed been used to launch wars (although the European Union has rendered wars within Western Europe unimaginable), the Kellogg Briand-Pact and the United Nations Charter have banned war, and wars have proceeded merrily on their way not noticing. But all of this criticism is overly simplistic. The United Nations is a corrupt approximation of an ideal never yet realized. And Outlawry, despite passage of the Kellogg-Briand Pact, has never been fully tried.

Outlawry, in Morrison's outline of it, requires that a world court ruling on a body of world law be substituted for war as a means of settling disputes. The international code of law (never produced by the Outlawrists) would, wrote Morrison, need to stipulate which disputes were international and under its jurisdiction and which types of disputes were domestic. The International Criminal Court (ICC), finally created in 2002 and having taken jurisdiction over the crime of aggression in 2010, begins to approach this idea, but the United States is not a member, and yet the court is under the thumb of the United States and the other permanent members of the U.N. Security Council. As things stand, the ICC will not prosecute aggression until 2017 at the earliest, and even then not against non-members such as the United States or in cases opposed by the U.N. Security Council. In fact, any war approved by the United Nations will, by the ICC's definition, not be aggression at all. The critics of the World Court as a creature of the League of Nations would, if brought forward in time, no doubt have a similar critique of the ICC as a creature of the United Nations.

Where the argument for Outlawry gets a little hairy is in its refusal to consider any distinction between aggressive and defensive war, while nonetheless countenancing armaments and self-defense. Morrison argues that distinguishing aggressors from defenders is a fool's errand, as every nation always claims to be fighting in defense, and an initial attack may have been provoked by the other side. (In 2001 and 2003 the United States attacked the distant, unarmed, impoverished nations of Afghanistan and Iraq and claimed to be acting in self-defense.) Morrison believes that self-defense will almost certainly not be needed, in the future of outlawed war, because war just won't happen. But were it to happen, self-defense clearly must be envisioned in Morrison's scheme as something that does not resemble war. For, otherwise, how can the world court of Outlawry determine which nation(s)' leaders to put on trial?

Ultimately, outlawing war is a process of moral development. Changing the law and establishing a court to enforce it are means toward changing people's conceptions of what is morally acceptable. Viewed in this way, the work of the 1920s that brought about the Kellogg-Briand Pact can be seen as a partial success to be built upon, whether or not any court will ever be able to both prosecute warmaking and avoid the distinction between aggression and defense.

Morrison argued that Outlawry was so clear and so popular that no statesman would dare oppose it. He urged popularizing the peace movement, taking it out of the hands of experts. And he was right about that. He was right about the United States and about the entire world. Nobody opposed banning war. Though we still have wars, most people do not want them. Wars may be Tyrannical Ruler Nature, or Corporate Profiteer Nature, but they are the furthest thing from Human Nature.

Morrison's book includes a draft treaty by Levinson. Although Morrison points out its simplicity relative to other attempts at peace, the draft is longwinded and repetitive in comparison with the final Kellogg-Briand Pact. This draft includes roughly the same language that ended up in the Pact, but it also includes language regarding the creation of a court.

It is the Oulawrists' analysis of what such a treaty would do that provides the real moral education, an education that has clearly reached only some of those it needs to reach. By banning war as an institution, Outlawrists hoped, first of all, to open the world's eyes to war's status as an institution. There was a dispute over whether war was legal or extralegal: Was it legally sanctioned or merely accepted like the weather? In either case, it was something that could be outlawed, but the evidence favored considering war to have been legal. "Society is not organized for peace," wrote Morrison; "it is actively organized for war."

> *The war system has a recognized and protected status in the social order, and there exists no peace system or institution which society recognizes and protects. This fact constitutes an awful moral abyss in our civilization for the modern conscience to contemplate. Peace talk when war is impending is hazardous for the talker, and in war time it is criminal. War talk in peace time, which is infinitely more wicked, runs no risk at all.*

Among those prosecuted for peace talk in 1917 was Eugene Debs, whose 10-year-sentence was never commuted by President Wilson, but was commuted in 1921 by President Warren G. Harding. Debs picked up 913,664 write-in votes for president as the Socialist Party candidate from his prison cell in 1920. In 1927, Morrison, foreshadowing President Dwight Eisenhower's critique of the military industrial complex in 1961, also cautioned that war possessed a profession that promoted its own ongoing existence, growth, and prestige, while threatening the rights of others.

I included in my book *War Is A Lie* a chapter called "Wars Are Not Legal" in which I pointed to the Kellogg-Briand Pact, the U.N. Charter, and other treaties and laws. I blog at a site called WarIsACrime.org. The uphill struggle these days is to convince anyone that war is illegal. But the pre-Kellogg-Briand Outlawrists struggled to make people aware that war was, at that time, legal and therefore needed to be outlawed. Levinson himself, to take the doctrine straight from the Socrates of Outlawry rather than from his Plato, wrote,

> *The principle underlying the outlawry of war is this: The law should always be on the moral side of every question. But the law of nations has always been on the wrong side of the war question. . . . For, what with laws of conscription, martial laws and espionage acts, everyone who impedes in the slightest degree the operations of war is a criminal. The dire effect of our present situation is plainly seen, for example, on our ministers of religion. They are all morally against war, but because it is legal multitudes of ministers find no way to oppose it. . . . The law which should condemn and stigmatize evil, actually embraces and nurtures it, and thereby thwarts the moral will of civilization. . . . [W]ar cannot be regulated or controlled, for it makes its own ruthless laws . . . ; therefore war must not be compromised with, but its entire system, with its warp of force and its woof of death, must be uprooted, overthrown, outlawed — abolished.*

The key word in all of this, I think, is 'stigmatize.' This is a moral objection from a lawyer to the status of war under the law.

He wants the law to rid itself of war in hopes that all of society will follow. This is a campaign subtly different from one aimed at immediately eliminating all war in an instant by the act of placing a criminal court system in its way. This is a campaign, in other words, which was destined to move as slowly as culture, and which we are obliged to advance as far as our own generation can advance it. Like slavery and duelling had, war had in the 1920s and still has in the twenty-first century a legal code dealing with how, not whether, to engage. The Kellogg-Briand Pact, the U.N. Charter, and the International Criminal Court's pending jurisdiction over the crime of aggressive war have added the beginnings of a legal code on whether to have war. Yet the code addressing how to have war still exists. Particular atrocities are lamented and prosecuted, while wars themselves are tolerated if not celebrated. But there has yet to be a war not replete with the most hideous atrocities. And there has yet to be a time when many or most of the earth's nations were not at peace. An atrocity-free war is far less likely than the establishment of permanent world peace.

GOOD FAITH

Morrison described Outlawry, not as isolationism, but as the creation of a world organization for peace, namely a court of law. But such a court was to differ from the Permanent Court of Arbitration or the World Court, the latter properly known as the Permanent Court of International Justice. It would not be a tribunal of arbitration, but rather a court of law ruling on a body of established law. And its rulings would not be enforced by sanctions. For Morrison, sanctions were the same evil as war, whether the sanctions involved military action or economic blockade. Instead, Outlawry would rely on the good faith of the world's nations, on what Morrison called "their plighted word."

This is, again, where the case for Outlawry strains the credence of many. If we could trust the good faith of the world's nations, why did we have war to begin with? And, moreover, if we could do so without any new structures for diplomacy or dispute resolution, what would we have changed? But the court envisioned by Outlawrists was, in fact, to be a forum of dispute resolution, not simply a forum for the prosecution of war makers. Disputes would be brought to court rather than to the battlefield. And to the extent that war was eliminated, the Outlawrists argued, the threat of war would be eliminated too, and with it the economic exploitation of weaker nations, and with that the hostile reactions we now refer to as blowback. The nations with the lowest domestic crime rates today are not those with the most law enforcement, but those that have found other approaches to reducing the societal factors contributing to crime. In addition, Morrison pointed out, relying on military alliances also meant nothing other than relying on the good faith of nations. With no one to enforce the enforcers' agreements, nations would go to war in defense of their allies if and only if they chose to do so. Such agreements, Morrison suggested, also missed the likelihood that an aggressor would not be a single nation but a group of them.

Finally Morrison returns to the central point. Enforcement of a ban on war through the tool of war leaves war planning in place. One cannot plan for war without increasing the likelihood of war, including wars launched to facilitate possible future wars. In 1927, the United States was engaged in Nicaragua, Morrison argued, because it saw the Panama Canal as a vital (or is that the wrong word?) war asset; it was engaged in Mexico because it wished to protect the Monroe Doctrine's ban on European war making in the Americas.

WAR WITHOUT AGGRESSION?

Theories of so-called just wars (*jus ad bellum*), with such wars often amounting to "defensive" wars, have been around since Aristotle, Cicero, Augustine, and Aquinas. Theories and laws on conduct during the course of wars (*jus in bello*) have been around since the Hebrew Bible and other ancient cultures. Both theories were advanced by influential authors such as Hugo Grotius — who published books on this topic in 1625 — and others from the Renaissance up through modern times. What was new with Outlawry was not the idea of applying laws to war, but the idea of banning all war, thus eliminating the need for *jus ad bellum* or *jus in bello*. All wars, and the entirety of all wars, would be illegal without distinction.

The idea that moral persuasion or economic pressure could enforce peace better than could war was not entirely new; the American Peace Society had espoused this position since 1828, as had Charles Sumner famously in a speech on the "True Grandeur of Nations" in Boston on July 4, 1845. Sumner's will had left a prize for an annual competition at Harvard for the best essay on how "war may be permanently superseded."

For much of U.S. history it was reasonable for citizens to believe, and they often did believe, that the U.S. Constitution banned aggressive war. Congress declared the 1846-1848 War on Mexico to have been "unnecessarily and unconstitutionally begun by the president of the United States." Congress had issued a declaration of war, but the House believed that President James Polk had lied to Congress. (President Wilson would later send troops to war with Mexico without a declaration.) It does not seem to be the lying that Congress viewed as unconstitutional in the 1840s, but rather the launching of an unnecessary or aggressive war.

In 1848 the U.S. Supreme Court ruled that the United States could not do what it nonetheless had just done: it could not gain Mexican territory by conquest. Inconsistency notwithstanding, this understanding of the U.S. Constitution was widespread. Chief Justice Roger Taney ruled that,

> *The country in question had been conquered in war, but the genius and character of our institutions are peaceful, and the power to declare war was not conferred upon Congress for the purpose of aggression or aggrandizement. . . . A war, therefore, declared by Congress, can never be presumed to be waged for the purpose of conquest or the acquisition of territory.*

In March 2003 Attorney General Lord Peter Goldsmith warned British Prime Minister Tony Blair in vain that "Aggression is a crime under customary international law which automatically forms part of domestic law," and therefore, "international aggression is a crime recognized by the common law which can be prosecuted in the U.K. courts." U.S. law evolved from English common law, and the U.S. Supreme Court recognizes precedents and traditions based on that law. U.S. law in the 1840s was closer to its roots in English common law than is U.S. law today, and statutory law was less developed in general; so it was natural for Congress to take the position that launching an unnecessary war was unconstitutional without needing to be more specific. In fact, just prior to giving Congress the exclusive power to declare war, the U.S. Constitution gives Congress the power to "define and punish Piracies and Felonies committed on the high Seas, and Offenses against the Law of Nations." At least by implication, this would seem to suggest that the United States was itself expected to abide by the "Law of Nations." In the 1840s, no member of Congress would have dared to suggest that the United States was not itself bound by the "Law of Nations." At that point in history, this meant customary international law, under which the launching of an aggressive war had long been considered the most serious offense, albeit one that was never criminally prosecuted.

Thanks to the Kellogg-Briand Pact and the U.N. Charter, we now have explicit and binding treaties prohibiting war, and — in the case of the Kellogg-Briand Pact — not just aggressive war but all war. And these treaties have been agreed to by the rest of the world. Article VI of the Constitution explicitly states,

This Constitution, and the Laws of the United States which shall be made in Pursuance thereof; and all Treaties made, or which shall be made, under the Authority of the United States, shall be the supreme Law of the Land; and the Judges in every State shall be bound thereby, any Thing

in the Constitution or Laws of any State to the Contrary
notwithstanding.

Even before the creation of the Kellogg-Briand Pact, nations used the justification that they were going to war to uphold the laws of war. Harold Lasswell pointed out in 1927 that a war could better be marketed to "liberal and middle-class people" if packaged as the vindication of international law. The British, he noted, had stopped arguing for World War I on the basis of national self-interest when they were able to argue against the German invasion of Belgium. The French quickly organized a Committee for the Defense of International Law. He continued,

> *The Germans were staggered by this outburst of affection for*
> *international law in the world, but soon found it possible to*
> *file a brief for the defendant. . . . The Germans . . . discovered*
> *that they were really fighting for the freedom of the seas and*
> *the rights of small nations to trade, as they saw fit, without*
> *being subject to the bullying tactics of the British fleet.*

The allies said they were fighting for the liberation of Belgium, Alsace, and Lorraine. The Germans countered that they were fighting for the liberation of Ireland, Egypt, and India. These were not arguments against war, but arguments for war by one's own side.

The idea of avoiding war by one's own side gained greater traction with World War I underway. Congress, then as now, passed so much verbiage that much of it was never noticed, even by Congress. When Senator Arthur Capper of Kansas, a key supporter of peace initiatives, introduced a resolution in support of Outlawry in 1927, he recalled in it that back on August 29, 1916, Congress had passed a bill including these words:

> *It is hereby declared to be the policy of the United States to adjust and settle its international disputes through mediation or arbitration, to the end that war may be honorably avoided.*

This was a statement of desire, rather than commitment, as it was followed by a proposal to create a court of arbitration that might render this ideal possible. But this language was moving in the right direction, as it aimed to avoid all war, a goal that became the topic of a veritable flood of books and pamphlets and speeches during the years leading up to passage of the Kellogg-Briand Pact.

U.S. Senator William Borah

SENATOR BORAH

The campaign for Outlawry, which has not yet ended, began on March 7, 1918, with S.O. Levinson's article in *The New Republic*. In February 1919, according to one version of events, Levinson read the Covenant of the League of Nations and immediately found it too weak to support, since it did not ban all war or establish a court to try the crime of war. Levinson proceeded to advise Republican Senator from Pennsylvania and former U.S. Attorney General and Secretary of State Philander Chase Knox of the political advantage of backing the Outlawry of war. On March 1, 1919, Senator Knox was the first to propose the Outlawry of war in the Senate. At this time, Levinson and Knox wanted a new league that would outlaw war and not use force. Opposition to the use of force was, at least in large part, Knox's influence on Levinson — who, as noted above, initially promoted the League of Nations. And in John Chalmers Vinson's telling it was Knox and other senators who talked Levinson out of lobbying for the League.

In December 1919 Levinson met with Senator William Borah who declared Levinson's plan for the Outlawry of war to be "masterly." At this time the Chair of the Senate Committee on Foreign Relations was Republican Senator Henry Cabot Lodge, the great grandson of Senator George Cabot, and the grandfather of Senator Henry Cabot Lodge Jr. The Senator Lodge of 1919 had promoted the Spanish American War as well as World War I. He would oppose the League and support a massive build-up of the Navy. His grandson would become a leading proponent of U.S. military adventurism in Central America and help maneuver the United States into a war in Vietnam where he would serve as U.S. Ambassador.

Lodge Sr. would die in 1924, at which point Borah would become the Chairman of the Senate Committee on Foreign Relations despite never having left the United States. Borah too would oppose the League, but he would become the leading proponent of Outlawry, for which he would first introduce a resolution in the Senate on February 13, 1923. That resolution would call for the outlawing of war, the codification of international law, and the creation of a world court. This would serve to counter President Harding's proposal that the United States join the World Court established by the League. Harding, too, opposed the League but felt pressure to do something for peace. Everyone would feel that pressure, and the something for peace would become, for everyone, Kellogg-Briand.

In contemporary terms in the area of foreign policy, William Borah was — in very rough comparison — Congressman Ron Paul of Texas, although he looked and spoke nothing like him and had far more power. Borah was an opponent of imperialism and militarism and resistant to internationalism of any sort. Borah was a conservative — not a religious or corporatist or militarist radical, but someone who was reluctant to embrace change. A later Chairman of the Senate Committee on Foreign Relations, also from Idaho and very much in Borah's tradition, was Senator Frank Church, a Democrat who served in the Senate from 1957 to 1981.

Borah initially gained fame in Idaho by preventing the lynching of a black man. He accomplished this by pretending to have two train cars full of militia, when in fact the train cars he'd brought to the scene were empty. Borah was elected to the U.S. Senate in 1907 and remained until he died in 1940. Also in 1907 Borah served as the unsuccessful prosecutor of labor leader Big Bill Haywood for alleged complicity in the murder of the former Governor of Idaho Frank Steunenberg.

Borah was not initially elected to the Senate as a crusader for peace. He was turned into one by the events of his time and by intense public pressure.

Senator Borah was an orator. People would pack the normally empty Senate galleries when they heard that he would be giving a speech. He was not humorous or entertaining but serious and passionate about what needed to be done. Will Rogers said that if Borah ever left the Senate, they might as well make stove wood of the seats in the gallery.

Borah was a Republican, but he often disagreed with the party. He opposed imperialism in Nicaragua by both Republican President Taft and Democratic President Wilson. He wanted a time limit set on the U.S. occupation of the Philippines. And yet he wanted an exemption from tolls for U.S. ships at the Panama Canal.

Borah was 52 when he began to take an interest in foreign policy, stimulated by events in Nicaragua and the Philippines. Some observers think he viewed foreign policy through a thick domestic lens. He came to oppose alliances and reject the use of force even to enforce a ban on the use of force. But Borah didn't begin with that position. He was always a work in progress.

In 1915, Borah wanted military action in Mexico and a larger Navy. In 1917 he supported World War I, demanding a victory but voting against a draft and favoring a tax of 80 percent on war profiteering. Borah later said that his vote for World War I was the one vote he regretted. He opposed the League of Nations and the World Court and considered the League's defeat in the U.S. Senate his greatest accomplishment. He then proposed that the United States and Japan and Britain take five years off from military shipbuilding. He supported negotiations on naval reductions but not treaties forming alliances.

Following World War I, Borah led the way in insisting that European nations pay their war debts. He blamed France for years for its militarism and its failure to pay its debts. In 1922 Borah refused to serve on a committee to welcome former French Prime Minister Georges Clemenceau to the United States. He also blamed England and others for not paying their war debts; he believed they would use the savings to build weapons, as they did — much as the United States uses borrowed funds to do today.

However, Borah wanted Russia and Germany brought into the community of nations. Importantly, he wanted Germany's crushing debt burden reduced to allow it "to pay and live." Borah came to favor disarmament and an end to secret alliances. He also wanted France to give up its claim on the Ruhr. On those conditions, Borah was willing to work with Europe for peace, but those conditions were not met, and meeting them was widely considered so impossible and insane as to reflect Borah's general distaste for foreign affairs. This led to the suggestion that once he'd become chair of the Committee on Foreign Affairs he would abolish foreign affairs altogether.

Yet Borah would be instrumental in expanding the Kellogg-Briand Pact to nations beyond France and the United States, and in getting it ratified by the U.S. Senate. Having opposed numerous peace proposals, Borah would back this one and would exercise great diplomacy in working with the French on it.

Borah always maintained that he wanted peace and wanted it in a manner "consistent with American traditions." Borah favored a war powers popular referendum, the idea of requiring a public vote before going to war being another idea of the time, but the Senator took no action to create it. Borah was, if nothing else, cautious. He wanted to do something new without really doing anything different. Vinson writes that "it was a veritable eye of the needle through which the policy of the nation would have to pass." Of course, Borah failed to do nothing new: the Kellogg-Briand Pact was dramatically new. It just impressed Borah as adhering to his principles. And its innovation fails to impress us today purely because it is routinely violated.

POST WAR PRELIMINARIES

Take away the gun
From ev-ry mother's son.
We're taught by God above
To forgive, forget and love,

The weary world is waiting for,
Peace, forevermore,
So take away the gun
From ev-ry mother's son,

And put an end to war.

—Al Jolson, in a December 2, 1920, letter to President-Elect Warren Harding.

The roaring twenties began with a clearing of the throat, the jazz age with a tuning of the instruments. These preliminaries included the defeat in late 1919 of League of Nations membership in the U.S. Senate. Levinson opposed the League because its Covenant did not outlaw war. He thought it would have passed the Senate if it had. Levinson advised Lodge on opposing the League, and campaigned hard against it — going so far as to write a version of Shakespeare's *Macbeth* in which the three witches are Lloyd George, Clemenceau, and Wilson, and the hell broth is the peace settlement. Levinson would have liked a compromise that added

the Outlawry of war, but many others would have still opposed
League membership, whether for reasons of principle or merely in
order to oppose President Wilson.

Levinson began urging Borah to run for president, but when
Harding was nominated Levinson lobbied him as well. Harding
spoke publicly in favor of outlawing war on September 4, 1920, and
two months later won a presidential landslide with his campaign
to bring back "normalcy." It was a month after the election that
Borah proposed that Japan, Great Britain, and the United States
reduce their naval building by 50 percent over the next five years.
Borah, who favored peace, low taxes, and a small military and
wanted a way to get there without the League of Nations, believed
he'd found a proposal to unite League supporters and opponents
and end war by eliminating weapons. In this calculation Borah
fell short, but the same framework would later lead to his support
for the Kellogg-Briand Pact. Wilson, of course, had favored
working through the League of Nations, and Harding (who would
be president from March 1921 to August 1923) was noncommittal
on disarmament.

Early in 1921 Senator Robert La Folette, a Republican/
Progressive from Wisconsin, began a study of war profits' relation
to war making. This eventually led to Senate investigations in the
1930s, but contributed to the public conversation in the meantime.
By June 1921 Borah had manage to introduce and pass a resolution
calling for his disarmament plan. Despite presidential coolness,
public support allowed that success which led to a conference
in Washington on naval disarmament between November 1921

and February 1922. The conference produced a treaty that Borah himself opposed on the grounds that it was an alliance and the product of secret diplomacy. The treaty was ratified nonetheless, and even Borah was glad to see this process shift opinion away from the necessity of the League of Nations. However, Borah came to see disarmament as hopeless, remarking that "Insincerity in disarmament has been reduced to a science."

Public opinion in the United States had traditionally opposed funding a standing military, and it continued to do so following World War I. The Army was reduced, in fact, to 175,000 personnel by 1921. Borah favored getting it down to 100,000.

Levinson tried to inject Outlawry into the Washington Disarmament Conference. He urged it on the French delegation. And the French publicly backed Outlawry, stating,

> *You want to outlaw the submarine and poison gas. We do not object. What we want however to get rid of is not this or that particular atrocity but the one great atrocity namely war itself. What France wants is to outlaw war, not this or that phase of war.*

This was in January 1922. But the conference did not seriously consider, and likely at this time the French did not seriously consider, Outlawry.

Levinson decided that he would have to go to the people of each country rather than their governments. He, therefore, launched a massive educational campaign through the American Committee for the Outlawry of War, formed on December 9, 1921, by a small group of dedicated people who would change the world, and 95 percent funded out of Levinson's pocket. The Committee published an Outlawry pamphlet on Christmas Day 1921.

During all of this period, Levinson and Dewey lobbied Borah to lead the Outlawry movement, and Borah resisted. Senator Capper sent the Outlawry pamphlet to his enormous mailing list. John Dewey wrote about Outlawry in *The New Republic*, as did John Haynes Holmes and Charles Clayton Morrison in their religious journals. According to Ferrell, Colonel Raymond Robins gave speeches "permeated with Biblical phraseology and millennial aspiration" that "frequently raised audiences to near-ecstatic heights. Every time the colonel went out on a circuit for Outlawry he left a trail of resolutions behind him." Churches and women's clubs loved Outlawry, which appealed to the record of having abolished not just slavery but also alcohol. Colonel Robins remarked: "We can outlaw this war system just as we outlawed slavery and the saloon." And yet, Senator Borah, a big proponent of prohibition and a big fan of Outlawry, continued to stall in the face of Levinson's relentlessly lobbying him to become the movement's public face.

In 1922, the Lion of Idaho slowly began to roar. In January, Levinson produced a pamphlet on Outlawry at Borah's request, and Borah republished it as a Senate document, placing it in the Congressional Record. Senators Borah and Capper mailed it to their lists.

Meanwhile, Raymond Robins barnstormed the country making speech after speech for Outlawry, and Levinson corresponded at length with anyone and everyone who expressed interest or raised objections. Organizations of all varieties passed countless resolutions in support of Outlawry. School boards and labor unions distributed pamphlets. Prominent figures gave their endorsements.

Groups that supported the Outlawry of war early in the campaign included some organizations that are still around today but which one cannot imagine even considering taking the same step again, even with the Kellogg-Briand Pact and the U.N. Charter already in existence and formally a part of our law. Among these were the National League of Women Voters, the Young Women's Christian Association, the National Association of Parents and Teachers, the Federal Council of Churches of Christ in America, and the American Legion.

It was at this time that the American Foundation was soliciting entries for its Bok Peace Plan Award. Many contestants who did not win sent their plans to Congress and to the State Department complaining of pro-League bias by the judges. Also at this time, Edward Filene sponsored a similar contest in France, Italy, Germany, and Great Britain, receiving 15,000 plans.

Come February 15, 1923, Borah finally introduced his Outlawry resolution in the Senate, following a tireless lobbying effort by Levinson. Borah, who was becoming internationally known as well as becoming a major national figure, now moved into the role of spokesman for Outlawry that Levinson needed.

Outlawry also began to unite peace groups in a way that the League and the Court did not. John Dewey wrote in support of Outlawry in a preface to Levinson's pamphlet and in March 2003 in *Foreign Affairs* and then twice in *The New Republic*. Dewey also spoke publicly on the topic of Outlawry. Borah, for his part, published two long articles on Outlawry in April 1923, one in the *New York Times* quoting Dewey at length, the other in the *Locomotive Engineers Journal* urging the acceptance of a unique U.S. responsibility to lead the world to peace. This sort of argument always makes a nice twist on the U.S. exceptionalism that so often has led to war.

Outlawry influenced the 1923 Draft Pact for Mutual Assistance and the 1924 Geneva Protocol for the Pacific Settlement of International Disputes without surviving in their texts in a form satisfactory to Levinson. Both of these League of Nations efforts failed to gain ratification by the nations of the world. Levinson considered both of them to be European in design. He found that "the way in which they would outlaw war is by war itself."

Amidst the ruins of the best-laid plans for world peace, the movement for Outlawry was rapidly expanding in the United States and abroad. Robins in 1923, Morrison in 1924, and Frances Keller in 1925 promoted Outlawry in Europe, where understanding and support for it would be needed if it were ever to be accomplished internationally.

A MOVEMENT GROWS AND UNITES

The peace movement growing in the 1920s developed in a nation different from the United States of the twenty-first century in many ways. One of them was the state of political parties. The Republicans and Democrats were not the only game in town. They were pushed in the direction of peace and social justice by the Socialist and Progressive Parties. By 1912, the Socialist Party, as recounted in John Nichols' 2011 book *The "S" Word* had elected 34 mayors and numerous city councilors, school board members, and other officials in 169 cities nationwide. In some states, the Socialist Party held the second highest number of seats in the legislature. The first Socialist was elected to Congress in 1911. By 1927, there would be one Socialist and three Minnesota Farmer-Labor Party members in Congress, along with a slim Republican majority in the Senate and a large Republican majority in the House.

When President Harding up and dropped dead in 1923, his vice president, Calvin Coolidge, got the top job and the Republican nomination to remain in it after 1924. Indeed, he remained until March 1929.

Levinson helped persuade Coolidge to pick Borah for the vice presidency and Borah to accept, but this deal fell through, Borah declined, and Charles Dawes accepted. Secretary of State Frank Kellogg would have occasion to refer to Dawes as "an unmitigated ass" prior to organizing the nations of the world in support of brotherly love. Borah would instead end up in the job of Chairman of the Senate Foreign Relations Committee.

Republican Wisconsin Senator Robert "Fighting Bob" La Folette pulled in the Socialist Party endorsement for president in 1924 and five million votes running under the banner of the Progressive Party. He won the state of Wisconsin, and nearly won North Dakota, Minnesota, and Montana. Another Progressive, U.S. Senator Hiram Johnson of California (he who famously said, "The first casualty, when war comes, is truth") had unsuccessfully challenged Coolidge for the Republican nomination. The Progressive Party Platform stated,

> *We denounce the mercenary system of foreign policy under recent administrations in the interests of financial imperialists, oil monopolists, and international bankers, which has, at times, degraded our State Department from its high service as a strong and kindly intermediary of defenseless governments to a trading outpost for those interests and concession-seekers engaged in the exploitations of weaker nations, as contrary to the will of the American people, destructive of domestic development, and provocative of war. We favor an active foreign policy to bring about a revision of the Versailles Treaty in accordance with the terms of the armistice, and to promote firm treaty agreements with all nations to outlaw wars, abolish conscription, drastically reduce land, air, and naval armaments, and guarantee public referendum on peace and war.*

Coolidge was a backer of World Court membership, but he was also in principle a supporter of Outlawry and of recognition for the Soviet Union. Outlawry made it into Coolidge's speech accepting the Republican nomination but not into the Republican Platform. It did, however, make it into the Democratic Party Platform.

The Abolition of War was published by Sherwood Eddy and Kirby Page in 1924. By 1924 Eddy, the former war enthusiast, supported conscientious objection, and Page was looking approvingly at Gandhi's work in India and, somewhat less so, at the nonviolent resistance of Germans in the Ruhr. Page argued for the League but also for Outlawry; he also argued for a public referendum power to precede any war declaration. Immune to the common disease that causes the favoring of one measure to somehow require the denunciation of all others, Page, in addition, favored a "conscription of wealth" in time of war, as a deterrent to war making.

In 1924 and 1925, with help from Charles Morrison, editor of *The Christian Century*, numerous religious groups declared themselves in support of Outlawry, including the Methodist General Conference and the Northern Baptist Convention. Harrison Brown, an Englishman in France, contacted Levinson and began promoting Outlawry in Europe.

Also in 1924, Levinson and the Outlawrists sought unity with fellow peace activists who supported the League, offering support for World Court membership in exchange for support for the Borah Resolution on Outlawry. Borah reintroduced his resolution on March 26, 1924. Pro-Leaguers James Shotwell, director of the Carnegie Endowment's Division of Economics and History; Frederick Keppel, president of the Carnegie Corporation; and William B. Hale, a publisher and banker, met with Levinson, Morrison, and Borah. Shotwell's side of this peace-within-the-peace-movement conference agreed to back Outlawry, but the Outlawrists had to recognize the recent work in Geneva (on the Protocol that was doomed to rejection by the British) and they had to accept an invitation to a Disarmament Conference called by the League of Nations. Unity was in the works, but it seems to have been found by ordinary activists more readily than by these leaders. Despite this bargaining, smooth relations among these men were not forthcoming.

The prolific Shotwell was a major force in the U.S. peace movement and would play a major role in recording the history of these times from the perspective of a mainstream U.S. peace advocate who favored the League and then supported the Kellogg-Briand Pact as well. Shotwell's books would include the following:

- *An Introduction to the History of History* (1922)
- *Plans and Protocols to End War* (1925)
- *War as an Instrument of National Policy* (1929)
- *The Origins of the International Labor Organization* (1934)
- *On the Rim of the Abyss* (1936)
- *At the Paris Peace Conference* (1937)
- *The Great Decision* (1944)
- *The Long Way to Freedom* (1960)

Shotwell, a U.S. history professor, had been born in Canada in 1874. He helped form the International Labor Organization in 1919, and he would go on to participate in the formation of the United Nations. His 1929 book *War As An Instrument of National Policy* makes concessions that I would not, and against which I have argued in *War Is A Lie*: that humans are "naturally" warlike, and that war has accomplished good things. But Shotwell favors the abolition of war and draws on the example of the abolition of slavery. "War," he writes, "which was once a directable [sic] instrument of policy has now changed its nature and ceases to be controllable and directable in the hands of statesmen. By reason of its all-embracing needs, it becomes a contagion among nations; and one cannot safely use a contagion as an instrument."

Shotwell points to one overwhelming factor that led to the Kellogg-Briand Pact: public demand. "The rising tide of public opinion, voiced in Congress by the Resolutions of Senator Capper and Senator Borah, and others in the House of Representatives, is directly responsible for the negotiations which led to the Pact of Paris." Shotwell also gives credit to public opinion in France, Great Britain, and Germany. But this was all before opinion polling became a common way to measure public opinion. Nor do any election results appear to have played a role in creating the idea of a public demand for renouncing war. While those struggling for women's suffrage had used marches and civil disobedience, and conscientious objectors to the World War I had used noncooperation, those were not the primary tools of this campaign. Instead there were numerous public meetings and packed lecture halls, signed petitions and resolutions. All of that activity was probably part of what Shotwell had in mind. But when Shotwell describes public opinion, he seems to equate it, quite straightforwardly, with the opinion of newspaper editorial boards. If newspaper editors favored outlawing war, then so did public opinion — either because newspapers simply are the public, or because newspapers represent the public. This seems either elitist or absurdly naïve today, but I suspect the newspapers did agree with most people in this case. And, in the end, it would be letters, telegrams, and lobby visits by at least a somewhat larger group of citizens that would close the deal.

Shotwell's most important colleague at the Carnegie Endowment for International Peace was its president Nicholas Murray Butler, who was also president of Columbia University. The *Philadelphia Record* in 1928 called him "the most lavishly decorated member of the human race." He had 38 honorary degrees, one *Time* magazine cover, and a two-part profile in the *New Yorker*. The *New York Times* printed his Christmas greeting to the nation every year. He was inducted into the Bricklayers, Masons, and Plasterers Union in 1923, and was elected president of the American Academy of Arts and Letters in 1928. Butler himself longed to be president of the United States and campaigned unsuccessfully for the Republican nomination in 1920 and 1928. In 1931 he would share the Nobel Peace Prize with Jane Addams.

On May 31, 1925, in Cleveland and June 3rd in New York, League and Outlawry backers met again to discuss cooperation. An agreement reached on June 26th backed adherence to the Court Protocol and within two years the backing of Outlawry and the holding of a conference to embody in a treaty the principles that war be made a crime and the Court be given jurisdiction. A third and final plank in this agreement was that the United States would withdraw from the Court if the Outlawry provisions were not put into effect within two years.

John E. Stoner, in the same book cited above, writes that he believes true supporters of Outlawry liked the agreement, as did Levinson, whereas those who merely used Outlawry to oppose other peace plans disliked it, as did Borah. Of course Borah may have just opposed the Court (this court, not any court) more than he supported Outlawry. Vinson records that Borah suspected this World Court would result in international alliances and would use force to impose its decisions. That was not only objectionable to someone like Borah, but it was also in direct conflict with Outlawry.

Borah' status as a holdout notwithstanding, this agreement, known as the Harmony Plan, really did help to bring the peace movement together. The plan, which is printed in Page's *An American Peace Policy*, was reported in national and international newspapers and served as a guide for local peace organizations, even though the peace movement leadership was back to quarrelling by December. "The Pact represented the efforts of all Americans," writes Vinson, "those that had favored the League of Nations as well as the most irreconcilable of its opponents. Isolationists were no less eager in their desire to establish peace than the most radical of the internationalists. The means but not the end were the subject of bitter debate."

It may be that the alliance of the left and the right, or rather of the internationalists and the isolationists, holds lessons for the future as well. Can libertarians who understand that diplomacy is far less costly than war find common ground with peace activists who recognize that tax cuts would be better than the military industrial complex? Two groups coming from very different perspectives united in the 1920s around a policy. They did not focus their concerns on a particular politician or party. They did not muddy the issue with concerns about whether to endorse entire ideologies. They did not engage in accusations of guilt by association. They found policies they could agree on and promoted those policies.

As the Senate considered the question of World Court membership, Levinson worked with Senator Borah, Senator Capper, and Republican Senator George Moses of New Hampshire. Capper, who voted in favor of the Court, declined to introduce a reservation related to Outlawry, so Moses — who openly opposed the Court — was recruited to do so. The reservation stated that the Court's opinions were "not to be enforced by war under any name or in any form whatsoever." Borah spoke at length about Outlawry during a debate on this Moses resolution, his eloquence widely and enthusiastically praised, but the reservation was not approved by the Senate. Levinson sent out 500,000 copies of Borah's speech and 600,000 of an earlier Borah address, resulting in 34,000 letters to Borah from Illinois alone.

In January 1926, the Senate voted to join the Court 76-17 but with several reservations making the United States virtually independent of the Court. The Court itself found the reservations unacceptable, and in November Coolidge announced that the United States would not be joining the Court. These difficulties were worked out eventually and the United States was able to join on March 4, 1929. However, President Herbert Hoover would fail to submit revised protocols for approval to the Senate, and it would be 1935 before President Franklin Delano Roosevelt would do so. At that time, the Hearst newspapers, Huey Long, and Father Coughlin would rage against the idea and defeat it for good. With the United States a non-member, American jurists would serve on the World Court, including Frank Kellogg from 1930-1935. But once the Senate had voted, in January 1926, the Court was no longer the focus of peace advocacy in the United States. The time for Outlawry to take the stage on its own was arriving.

Shotwell would conclude that the Court ultimately failed while the Kellogg-Briand Pact succeeded, as a result of public opinion. The Court was too technical and complicated by numerous reservations for the public to rally behind it. And the Court was seen as a backdoor into the League.

Levinson, like the peace movement, had been racking up failures. He'd lost an effort to prevent European debt settlements. He had hoped to use the leverage of those debts to extract commitments to Outlawry. He'd lost in his efforts to defeat the Court outright in the Senate, efforts which he had pursued despite the Harmony Plan, as well as in his efforts to attach Outlawry to the Court. He had failed to persuade Borah to make the Outlawry speech he wanted in the Senate. But Levinson made good use of the speeches Borah did make and moved on, proposing a new campaign to withdraw from the Court unless its signatories outlawed war by 1928. Levinson's colleagues refused to back such a plan, preferring to end the peace movement's infighting.

Senator Borah turned his attention to defending the prohibition of something else: alcohol. He and Butler would famously debate the topic on April 8, 1927, with Butler arguing for prohibition to be repealed. That debate would take place two days after the first move was made to create the Kellogg-Briand Pact by French Foreign Affairs Minister Aristide Briand. Butler met with Briand in June 1926, at which point Briand asked "What can we do next?" Butler replied: "My dear Briand, I have just been reading a book . . . . Its title is *Vom Kriege*, and its author was Karl von Clausewitz . . . . I came upon an extraordinary chapter in its third volume, entitled 'War as an Instrument of Policy.' Why has not the time come for the civilized government of the world formally to renounce war as an instrument of policy?" Briand's reply was "Would not that be wonderful if it were possible? I must read that book."

French Foreign Minister Aristide Briand

ARISTIDE BRIAND

Many French towns have a street named for Aristide Briand. But who was he? Briand was born in 1862 in Nantes where he became good friends with Jules Verne. He studied law and entered politics, supporting the formation of trade unions and helping to lead the French Socialist Party. He was elected to the Chamber of Deputies in 1902 and successfully drafted and passed a law on the separation of church and state. Briand became Prime Minister of France in 1909, and would serve in that office 11 times, off and on, while also serving repeatedly as Foreign Minister, including during the period from 1925 to his death in 1932. Briand shared the 1926 Nobel Peace Prize with German Foreign Minister Gustav Stresemann in recognition of their work at Locarno. France and Germany's friendly relationship, as led by Briand and Stresemann, would end with their deaths in 1932 and 1929 respectively.

A cartoon once depicted the statesmen of the world smashing a statue of Mars while Briand, alone, talked to the god of war trying to convince him to commit suicide. Briand was an enemy of war and an advocate of personal diplomacy. He was neither a reader nor a writer. He was a listener and a brilliant speaker who did not prepare his speeches ahead of time. He did, however, write for newspapers, preferring journalism to the practice of law. Briand wrote for *Le Peuple, La Lanterne, La Petite République*, and collaborated with Jean Jaurès in founding *L'Humanité*, a socialist paper.

Briand got himself expelled from the Socialist Party by joining the Sarrien government in 1906. And he broke a railway workers' strike in 1910 by conscripting the workers into the military. Briand was Prime Minister during part of World War I, from October 1915 to March 1917. He devised a successful military venture, striking Turkey, Bulgaria, and Austria through Greece, and helped to obtain a new ally in Italy. But Briand was not part of the Clemenceau government that negotiated the Treaty of Versailles.

In 1925, at Locarno, Briand welcomed Stresemann's offer of a pact of mutual guarantee and nonaggression. Briand showed Austen Chamberlain how this proposal would fit into his concept of regional, collective security pacts. And Briand was credited with creating an atmosphere of informal amiability that brought about agreement. The Locarno Pact included four arbitration treaties between Germany on the one hand and France, Belgium, Poland, and Czechoslovakia on the other, and two treaties between France on the one hand and Poland and Czechoslovakia on the other. Germany's western boundaries were guaranteed, the Rhineland was to be demilitarized, war was renounced except in extraordinary circumstances, and Germany was to join the League of Nations.

With Locarno as his model, Briand sought to extend the arbitration concept to the United States, making a proposal that we will come to momentarily.

Briand also, perhaps most significantly (but this is a topic for another book), proposed a European Union in a May, 1930, memo to 26 nations.

A PLAN COMES TOGETHER

In 1927 the pressure on world leaders to take steps to ensure peace reached a climax, and the pieces of a plan began to be fitted into place. Morrison's *The Outlawry of War*, James Brown Scott's *The Judicial Settlement of International Disputes*, and Thomas Hall Shastid's *Give the People Their Own War Power* were among the many books on peace published in that year. Shastid described war as the worst known disease in need of a cure.

Political organizations and clubs pushing for peace were springing up by the hundreds, and the question of the League of Nations was no longer there to divide them. Until now, in Shotwell's words, "the failure to accept the League drove a wedge into liberal opinion and split the peace movement into small groups of bitter, partisan sectaries, too busily engaged in warring among themselves to do anything effective for peace itself." But unification was made possible in 1927.

The peace movement for the time being had ceased to confuse the popular mind with conflicting claims and doctrinal discussions. The peace movement had been largely futile in the United States, not because of any general lack of support for the main principles which it upheld, but because of its inability to decide how peace was actually to be attained. Now that there was a common agreement in support of the simple proposition that the United States should join in a

renunciation of war as an instrument of policy, the peace
forces gained rapidly in influence throughout the country at
large. This became evident not only in the press but in public
meetings which were held all over the country.

In 1927, in response to public demand, Senators Capper and Borah and Republican Representative Theodore Burton of Ohio would introduce resolutions that would make national and international news. Burton's resolution proposed a ban on U.S. shipments of arms to nations that made aggressive war. The Navy's program of building was also an area of heated opposition from the peace movement — opposition that ended up serving as energy in support of the Kellogg-Briand Pact.

In March of 1927, Shotwell was the Visiting Carnegie Professor of International Relations at the Hochschule für Politik in Berlin. Shotwell delivered a lecture attended by the German chancellor, his cabinet, and the War Office staff, in which he argued that war no longer profited a nation and that nations should abolish it as a means of policy. Shotwell and his friend Albert Thomas went to Paris to meet Briand on March 22nd. France had just refused a U.S. invitation to a disarmament conference. France was still upset both about its treatment at the conference in Washington and about U.S. accusations of militarism, not to mention U.S. insistence on war debt payment, and U.S. refusal to join the League or the Court. Shotwell suggested removing U.S. suspicions of French militarism by proposing a treaty to renounce war as an instrument of national policy.

On April 6, 1927, Levinson was on a train to New York where he would sail to Europe. He read the day's newspapers on the train and was overjoyed and overwhelmed by an Associated Press report of a public statement from Briand, the Foreign Minister of France. Shotwell later told both John Dewey and Robert Ferrell that he had written Briand's message himself. The message actually began by praising U.S. participation in war, the United States having entered World War I 10 years earlier:

> *At this hour when the thought of the Western World reverts to that solemn date of the entrance of the United States into the war, I address to the American people the warm expression of cordial fraternity and complete confidence which the French people will always cherish for them.*
>
> *I cannot forget that I was the first to learn, through an official communication from Mr. Sharp, then Ambassador of the United States at Paris, that the Federal Government had reached the decision which was to exert so considerable an influence on the history of the World War.*
>
> *Ten years have passed since the American nation, with magnificent enthusiasm, associated itself with the Allied Nations for the defense of imperiled liberty and in the course of those years the same spirit of justice and humanity has continued to inspire our two countries, both determined to put an end to the war and to prevent its return.*

Briand then builds his case that France is not militarist. (In

2003, with the U.S. government eager to attack Iraq, France was deemed insufficiently militarist; there's no pleasing everybody.)

France wishes to live in an atmosphere of confidence and peace and the evidence of this is her signature to agreements tending to hold at bay the threat of conflict. Limitation of armaments, sincerely sought by both of our governments, meets the ardent desires of the entire French people on whom heavy military charges have weighed for more than half a century and who for four years suffered devastation, not yet repaired.

After recounting France's disarmament efforts, Briand shifts topics:

More important than any question of procedure in the technical elaboration of a plan for disarmament is the question of the policy of peace, that is to say the will to peace and the habit of thinking in terms of peace. For after all disarmament can only result from the will to peace of the nations of the civilized world and it is on this point that American thought is always sure to be in agreement with French thought.

And now Briand makes an offer that will dominate the global campaign for peace during the coming months:

For those whose lives are devoted to securing this living reality of a policy of peace the United States and France already appear before the world as morally in full agreement. If there were need for those two great democracies to give high testimony to their desire for peace and to furnish to other peoples an example more solemn still, France would be willing to subscribe publicly with the United States to any mutual engagement tending 'to outlaw war,' to use an American expression, as between these two countries. The renunciation of war as an instrument of national policy is a conception already familiar to the signatories to the Covenant of the League of Nations and of the Treaties of Locarno. Every engagement entered into in this spirit by the United States toward another nation such as France would contribute greatly in the eyes of the world to broaden and strengthen the foundations on which the international policy of peace is being erected. These two great friendly nations, equally devoted to the cause of peace, would furnish to the world the best illustration of the truth that the immediate end to be attained is not so much disarmament as the practical application of peace itself.

This was public diplomacy at its most public. The Foreign Minister of France was proposing a treaty through the Associated Press. The only downside to such methods was that a response could not be required. And in fact, no response from the U.S. government was forthcoming. And the newspapers didn't see any story worth pursuing. On April 8th Butler and Borah publicly debated the outlawing of rum, which was of much more interest to the media. Butler, who wanted to abolish war believed banning rum was too difficult. With regard to Briand's offer, Butler took matters into his own hands. The Columbia University President published a letter in the *New York Times* on April 25, 1927, demanding action in response to Briand's proposal.

Butler's letter in the *New York Times* and a supportive editorial published by the *New York Times* caught the wider news media's attention. Newspapers turned it into a big story in the United States and even abroad. Butler's letter attempted to shame the United States' government:

> *The question is now squarely before the people of the United States. If those moral forces to which M. Briand makes appeal do not really exist among us, or, if existing, they cannot secure such direction of our policies as shall realize these ideals, then in international relations we shall have reached a stage which no American who understands his country's traditions and who realizes his country's ideals can look upon without shame and sorrow. . . . M. Briand, speaking the voice and expressing the soul of France, has called out to us across the ocean. What answer is he to hear? What evidence is he to have that these noble words have been heard and understood?*

This was Butler beginning a dialogue with his colleague Shotwell, but with Butler speaking for the United States and Shotwell having spoken through Briand for France. Not a bad bit of ventriloquism. Shotwell would later write about Butler's letter:

The reception given this letter was something more than a complete justification of the persistence of the American government; it was even a justification of public diplomacy. The outburst of popular approval which it called forth throughout the whole world showed that the public opinion of democracies is in advance of the cautious policy of their governments.

More speakers were quickly added to the discussion. Numerous senators spoke up in support of answering Briand's offer. Borah, however, was silent. A May 2, 1927, *New York Times* editorial asked when Borah would speak. That same evening Shotwell spoke in New York at the League of Nations Non-Partisan Association which then passed a resolution approving Briand's proposal. In response, Borah commented, but he was noncommittal. Meanwhile, the White House and the State Department were silent, rumored to be piqued that Briand had spoken directly to the people of the United States, and taking the position when asked that no response was required as nothing had officially been communicated.

The U.S. government did not, however, choose to prosecute Shotwell under the Logan Act. This law makes it a felony punishable by six months to three years in prison to seek to influence a foreign government in its relations to the United States. The law had been put on the books in 1799 after a peace activist named George Logan in 1798 had engaged in his own peace negotiations with France.

In Germany, support was strong. "No other Great Power in the world today has made such a radical change in its attitude towards peace and war as Germany," wrote Shotwell. He continued,

> *The new German Republic is an unprecedented experiment in the politics of peace. Shorn of armaments by the Treaty of Versailles and deprived for the time being of the reassertion of its military and naval power, it has been forced from the very exigencies of its post-war situation to find and apply the practical equivalents in terms of peace for the arbitrament [sic] of the sword. It has concentrated upon this task both theoretically and practically, and the new German Republic is a laboratory for the study of pacific international affairs, such as the modern world presents nowhere else.*

That this changed in the coming years doesn't mean it was completely wrong. It fairly accurately describes the Germany that would arrive after the Second World War as well.

On May 4th, 1927, Levinson arrived in Paris, having gone to England on the way. Right away, Levinson and Harrison Brown met with Alexis Leger, aide to Briand. The question of aggressive war arose immediately. Levinson answered Leger's question with a series of questions. Levinson asked Leger whether France considered Germany the aggressor in the World War, and whether Germany considered Russia the aggressor, and whether Russia considered Austria the aggressor. Yes, yes, yes, replied Leger. The point, of course, whether correct or not, was that an aggressor cannot always be identified and agreed upon.

Thomas Hall Shastid made a similar point, arguing in 1927 for a public referendum before the launching of any war. He was asked why the Constitutional Amendment that he was proposing did not specify "aggressive war." Shastid replied: "Because that would leave to Congress the decision as to whether or not any proposed war was 'defensive' or 'aggressive,' and, of course, if the powers which control Congress wanted a war, the war would always be called a 'defensive' war, no matter where waged or under what circumstances."

Briand later told Levinson: "I have never known my Leger to give his confidence to any man so quickly and so fully as he did to you." Levinson also met with the American Ambassador to France. By May 8th, he was cabling allies back home, including Borah, that France was ready to outlaw war. On May 9th, Senator Borah talked up the idea in a speech in Cleveland. Also on May 9th, Senator Thomas Walsh of Montana praised Briand's April 6th statement in a speech in Paris. Levinson showed Leger a resolution passed by a large U.S. peace group asking President Coolidge to respond to Briand's proposal. Briand very much wanted approval from Coolidge, but Levinson presented Leger with the next best thing — U.S. press clippings showing public pressure on Coolidge.

A few days after Butler's letter in the *New York Times*, the American Foundation proposed a draft treaty. Then professors Shotwell and Joseph Chamberlain of Columbia University proposed a draft treaty, as did Francis Bowes Sayre of Harvard. These proposals made international news. The treaties being proposed were exclusively between France and the United States.

Senator Borah's reluctance to join this movement was due to his distaste for bilateral alliances. He was not interested in signing on to go to war for France the next time France attacked or was attacked. Borah favored a multilateral treaty in which all the world's nations, without particular alliances, would agree to outlaw war. On May 4th, Borah made his first public statement on Briand's offer proposing that Briand turn it into a draft treaty. The *New York Times* praised Borah for this statement. Five days later, Borah gave a speech in Cleveland proposing that Briand's idea be extended to all countries.

And still, Briand had not yet contacted the U.S. State Department through official acceptable channels, and the U.S. Secretary of State Frank Kellogg had yet to show any interest in the matter at all.

U.S. Secretary of State Frank Kellogg

FRANK B. KELLOGG

Frank B. Kellogg served the people of a representative republic by representing them. He was not elected or appointed to office as a crusader for peace. He was pushed into becoming one, a result that speaks well of him but even better of the U.S. public.

L. Ethan Ellis, in his 1961 book *Frank B. Kellogg and American Foreign Relations, 1925-1929*, describes Kellogg as "slight (five feet six inches), inclined to stoutness, snowy-haired, and afflicted with a tremor of hands and head, as well as one artificial eye. He possessed a temper which flared in sudden violence and as quickly subsided. Somewhere he had acquired the nickname of 'Nervous Nellie,' whether because of his physical handicaps and excitable temperament, or because of his habit of vacillating rapidly in reaching a decision, cannot now be determined. Addicted to vigorous physical exercise, he was perhaps the most ardent and accomplished golfer ever to hold the Secretaryship. . . . There is ample evidence, too, that he enjoyed the amenities connected with the so-called 'nineteenth hole,' despite the limiting factor of the Eighteenth Amendment."

Robert Ferrell's description in 1952 was similar: "Physically a small person with gnarled and shaking hands, white-haired, seventy years of age in 1927." Secretary of State Frank Kellogg was "noted for his industry and also his explosive and often profane temper. Especially the temper."

Kellogg first became known as a trustbuster. In 1904, President Theodore Roosevelt asked Kellogg to prosecute General Paper Company as a combination of companies that was restraining trade. Kellogg won the case, and then another against E. H. Harriman and the Union Pacific Railroad, and a third in 1911 against John D. Rockefeller and the Standard Oil Company. In 1912 Kellogg was named president of the American Bar Association.

Kellogg was a Republican and was elected in 1916 to the U.S. Senate from Minnesota. He voted in favor of entering World War I and initially supported the failed effort to ratify the Treaty of Versailles and the Covenant of the League of Nations. Kellogg came to believe the treaty needed reservations attached to it. When such a compromise proved unworkable, Kellogg turned against joining the League. He voted Aye with reservations, and Nay without.

Kellogg was a U.S. Senator from March 4, 1917, to March 4, 1923, during which time the U.S. military was engaged in World War I and in operations in Russia, Panama, Cuba, the Dominican Republic, Haiti, Mexico, Honduras, Yugoslavia, Guatemala, West Virginia, Turkey, and China. On February 7, 1919, Kellogg voted to bring to the floor a resolution "expressing the Senate's opinion that U.S. soldiers be withdrawn from Russia as soon as possible." On October 10, 1921, Kellogg voted for free tolls for U.S. ships through the Panama Canal. I've seen no record of any extraordinary advocacy for peace by Senator Kellogg.

Kellogg failed to win reelection for a second term. So, in 1923, President Harding sent him on his first diplomatic mission as a delegate to the fifth Pan-American Conference. Then President Coolidge nominated Kellogg as ambassador to the United Kingdom, where he served for 14 months, taking part in the London Reparations Conference convened to accept the Dawes Committee report.

In 1925, Coolidge nominated him for Secretary of State, where he remained until 1929. Kellogg's relative restraint in imperialistic militarism during this period in Mexico, Nicaragua, the Caribbean, South America, and China, would later be praised by the Nobel Prize Committee. However, during Kellogg's tenure as Secretary of State, the U.S. Marines went into Panama, Honduras, and Nicaragua. As Ellis recounts, Kellogg employed the threat of war to pressure Mexico in the interest of U.S. corporations, pointing out to the Mexican Ambassador that the U.S. government had the option of ceasing to embargo arms shipments to Mexican revolutionaries, while also threatening that passage of a Petroleum Law that sought to keep Mexican resources for Mexico "might adversely affect the cordiality of the relations between the two Governments."

Some months into the job, Kellogg was described by H.L. Mencken as a "doddering political hack from the cow country." By January 4, 1927, the *Baltimore Sun* was calling him "a discredited foreign minister" who, "whipped by the diplomatists of every banana republic, publicly ridiculed by the Bolshevists, denounced by candid men among his own countrymen . . . now runs to earth and hides in sullen silence behind a door closed to representatives of the press. . . ."

Nonetheless, Kellogg signed bilateral arbitration treaties with 19 nations, and signed a total of 80 treaties of all kinds, breaking the previous record set by William Jennings Bryan. From 1930 to 1935 he would serve on the Permanent Court of International Justice.

Kellogg's authorized biography by David Bryn-Jones, in the production of which Kellogg participated, states: "And of all the experiences and recollections of those years, none shine out more brightly in retrospect than those that were connected with the project which Mr. Kellogg always regarded as the consummation and crown of his labors — the Pact of Paris."

In 1937, Kellogg established for Carleton College in Minnesota the Frank B. Kellogg Foundation for Education in International Relations with a $500,000 endowment. The endowment initially funded two full-time professors and one half-time professor and provided scholarships for six students. Carleton College is where future U.S. Senator Paul Wellstone would teach from 1969 to 1990.

A self-guided tour book at the National Cathedral in Washington, D.C., describes one bay and window of the cathedral: "Kellogg Bay is a memorial to diplomat and statesman Frank B. Kellogg and reflects his ardent desire for universal peace. On the east wall is a carving of the Rev. Dr. Martin Luther King, Jr., preaching his last Sunday sermon from the Cathedral's pulpit (March 31, 1968)."

Below the Kellogg window at the National Cathedral, where his ashes are buried, is this inscription:

IN GRATEFUL MEMORY OF
FRANK BILLINGS KELLOGG, LL.D.
1856-1937
SENATOR OF THE UNITED STATES FROM MINNESOTA
AMBASSADOR TO THE COURT OF ST. JAMES
SECRETARY OF STATE
A JUDGE OF THE PERMANENT COURT OF
INTERNATIONAL JUSTICE
JOINT AUTHOR OF THE KELLOGG-BRIAND PACT
IN FIDELITY TO AMERICAN IDEALS
HE SERVED HIS NATION
WITH CONSPICUOUS ABILITY
AND SOUGHT
EQUITY AND PEACE
AMONG THE NATIONS OF THE WORLD
HIS BODY RESTS IN THIS CATHEDRAL

Interestingly, when Kellogg first read Butler's letter in the *New York Times*, he told a friend, George Barton, that Butler and the French were a set of "_____ fools" making suggestions that could lead to nothing but embarrassment. If there was anything he hated, Kellogg said, it was "_____ _____ pacifists."

But a year later, as prospects of bringing the entire world to outlaw war would appear within reach, Kellogg would do everything he could to make that happen. He would write to his wife: "If I can only get that treaty made, it will be the greatest accomplishment of my administration or of any administration lately." He enclosed a newspaper clipping suggesting his name for a Nobel Peace Prize. "If I could only get that treaty through," he wrote, "I think quite likely I would get that prize."

Here was someone seeking fame and prestige for all the right reasons, reflecting well on himself and his society. The state of affairs in 1927 when Kellogg was denouncing the peace activists is easily recognizable to us in the early twenty-first century. The part of the story that needs explaining to us is the state of affairs in 1928 when government officials had begun putting in the sort of energy working for peace that is usually invested only by peace activists. Why were government officials behaving exactly as if they really gave a damn about human life (and Nobel prizes)?

There was a presidential election coming. The clock was ticking on Kellogg's government career. The electoral and communication systems were less corrupt than today. But primarily there was a stronger peace movement.

That, and on May 21, 1927, Charles Lindbergh landed an airplane in France.

THE FRENCH CONNECTION

Ongoing illegal diplomacy by U.S. citizens in France got a boost from Charles Lindbergh's May 20-21, 1927, solo flight from New York to Paris.

U.S. Ambassador to France Myron Herrick wrote to Kellogg that Lindbergh's flight had done more to improve Franco-American relations than years of effort by diplomats. That had, in fact, been the goal of the Frenchman, Raymond Orteig, who had offered a $25,000 prize for a transatlantic flight. Had Lindbergh not made it, the result might have been similar, if not as large. Two French aviators had left Paris a few days earlier for New York but not arrived. That tragedy was already bringing the two nations together when Lindbergh succeeded. "Lindbergh had valorously shown that the 'impossible' was possible. Idealists everywhere began to take heart," wrote Ferrell. On May 26 Briand hosted a lunch for Lindbergh at which he told Herrick he wanted to speak with him in a few days about the possible treaty.

Needless to say (well, O.K., it isn't needless to say, but I wish it were) I am mentioning Charles Lindberg's name here without endorsing every action he took in his life, and certainly not his later fondness for Nazism, which I discussed in my earlier book *War Is A Lie.*

Meanwhile, back in Washington, D.C., Butler met with Undersecretary of State Robert Olds, who also happened to be a trustee of the Carnegie Endowment for International Peace. Olds told Butler that the State Department had no plans to reply to Briand. Butler told Olds that the State Department should reply and should reply with a draft treaty. Olds asked Butler to draft it. Butler then asked Shotwell and Joseph P. Chamberlain to help. Shotwell showed a draft to Olds, who approved. Shotwell sent Olds the final draft on May 25, letting him know he would give it to the U.S. and European press the next week and that he hoped the public response would help.

The positive interest in Germany, including from the German government, was not helping in France. And the British press was cold to the whole idea. But French Foreign Minister Briand was fully engaged. That next week Briand raised the matter again with the U.S. ambassador Herrick suggesting that they get to work before outsiders could interfere. Yet the *New York Times* reported on the same day on which Briand spoke to Herrick, that Briand favored something simpler than the Shotwell-Chamberlain draft, and that he believed the more public discussion devoted to the Outlawry proposal the easier it would be for governments to act. It seems Briand may have actually wanted outsiders to interfere, and the more of them the better. Briand's chief of staff Alexis Leger led Shotwell and Butler, on the one hand, and Levinson on the other, to believe that they and not their rival were part of the process. The message to Herrick was that none of these peace activists were part of the process. Nothing could have been further from the truth.

Levinson was touring Europe promoting Outlawry and receiving a good welcome, except from the British Foreign Office; it refused his request for a meeting by declaring that "the outlawry of war is all buncombe." In fact, Levinson proposed not only to outlaw war, but also to delete Article 231 (placing guilt for World War I entirely on Germany) from the Treaty of Versailles, and to settle all war debts. Presumably this was all more buncombe as far as the British Foreign Office was concerned. Levinson got on much better with the French Foreign Ministry. According to Harrison Brown, on or about May 23, 1927, Levinson scribbled two sentences on an envelope and handed it to Leger. They were the two sentences that became the Kellogg-Briand Pact.

However, even Levinson was, at this point, thinking in terms of a bilateral treaty between France and the United States. Senator Borah for his part was focused on opposing U.S. imperialism in Nicaragua and Mexico. This had the benefit of putting Coolidge and Kellogg on the defensive. Arthur Ponsonby of the English House of Commons declared his willingness to offer a resolution like Borah's on Outlawry. But Borah himself was stalling. So was the U.S. State Department.

On June 3, 1927, J. Theodore Marriner drafted an internal State Department memo for William Richards Castle, Jr. Marriner was chief of the Division of Western European Affairs. Castle, who had been born in Hawaii, where his father and grandfather had grown wealthy colonizing, had been appointed Assistant Secretary of State on February 26, 1927. Four days after the memo was drafted, the *New York Times* reported that the State Department believed the renewal of an expiring Root arbitration treaty with France (that is, a treaty that had been negotiated by former Secretary of State Elihu Root) would be all that was needed. The next day, the *New York Times* reported that for fear of a negative military alliance with the single nation of France, the U.S. government would need all the great powers to sign an Outlawry proposal.

On June 10th, Butler arrived in France. He found that Briand favored a simple declaration not to resort to war. Also that day, Secretary of State Kellogg read in the *New York Times* that Briand had given Herrick a note on how to frame the treaty. Kellogg cabled Herrick who said he'd been given no such note. Kellogg told Herrick to tell Briand they'd be glad to negotiate and that it should be done through the French Ambassador in Washington. That ambassador was then in France, so Kellogg had effectively delayed things for some weeks — or tried to.

On June 14, 1927, Levinson, returning from Europe, arrived in the United States. John E. Stoner's *S. O. Levinson and the Pact of Paris*, a book that is otherwise often quite critical, sums up rather hagiographically the work that confronted Levinson at this point:

> *The labors of Levinson, like those of Hercules, appeared to increase in difficulty in geometric ration after he arrived in his native land. However, unlike Hercules, he had only three. He had to educate and convert the cautious Kellogg and the inert Coolidge; to convince his lieutenants that the Briand proposal was not venom; and to transmute their constitutional obstructionist attitude into one of co-operation and support. The captain of the hosts of outlawry*

had to keep a watchful eye not only on the enemy but also on his own soldiers, each of whom carried a marshal's baton in his knapsack. [Martial analogies survived the outlawing of war quite well.] And he had to prevent the Briand proposal from being changed by its friends or foes in such a way that any agreement arising out of it would be defeated in the Senate or be a violation of the principles of outlawry.

On June 16, 1927, Butler gave a speech to the American Club in Paris. He proposed three short paragraphs that could be learned by children in schools: renouncing war as an instrument of policy, accepting the Locarno definition of an aggressor, and agreeing not to aid an aggressor in case of war. According to Harrison Brown, who was working for Levinson, Briand was responsible for this shift in Butler toward clarity, simplicity, and popularization.

Also on June 16th, Levinson met with Secretary of State Kellogg for 45 minutes and found him "quite unacquainted with the theory of Outlawry and considerably in the dark as to what M. Briand really wanted." Kellogg also met with Borah, who began to inform him about Outlawry.

On June 20, 1927, a Coolidge Naval Disarmament Conference opened in Geneva, Switzerland, without France participating. The conference ended in failure on the 27th.

Also on June 20th Briand finally got around to making a proposal through the proper acceptable channels. He drafted a proposed treaty. In contrast to the rest of Briand's approach, the text of this proposal would not be made public until much later on January 11, 1928. On June 21, 1927, Philippe Berthelot, Secretary General of the French Ministry of Foreign Affairs, told Sheldon Whitehouse, U.S. Charge d'Affaires in Paris and grandfather of the eponymous twenty-first-century U.S. senator, that because it would be the end of August before the French Ambassador reached Washington, Briand had gone ahead and drafted a treaty. Whitehouse cabled a translation to Washington. The next day, Briand's office informed the media, without providing the text of the treaty, and described it as a simple treaty between only two countries. The draft in fact contained two short statements renouncing war as an instrument of national policy and avowing to settle disputes only with peaceful means. It was similar to treaties France had made with other countries, and it named only France and the United States. It was otherwise quite close to the final Kellogg-Briand Pact.

Butler went on a speaking tour of the United States. Levinson worked to fill the newspapers of the Midwest with positive coverage. Through 1927 in the United States, daily and weekly small-town newspapers, especially in the Midwest, were pushing forward the idea of an Outlawry treaty. They would come to back Briand's proposal increasingly through the year as further developments reduced suspicions of the French and the treaty was enlarged to include more nations.

In Britain, too, some newspapers now backed the idea of an Outlawry treaty enthusiastically. Meetings were held all over the country and resolutions passed supporting it. But the British government delayed. A proposal was discussed in Parliament of calling for an international conference of experts to draft the treaty. Italy, represented by Benito Mussolini, and Japan would each also end up proposing that an international conference of experts handle the matter. The U.S. State Department expressed its opposition to that plan.

In Kellogg's papers is a June 22, 1927, letter from U.S. Senator Irvine L. Lenroot of Wisconsin sending him both a proposed treaty by the American Foundation published in *Foreign Affairs* and a May 1927 pamphlet by the American Foundation. The proposed treaty would have referred disputes to the World Court. Also included was a proposed joint congressional resolution requesting that the President consider the treaty. A thank you letter from Kellogg was sent back the same day.

Scrolling further through Kellogg's papers on the microfilm at the University of Virginia, I read a June 24th memo from Marriner warning against forming an obligation to France and urging a universal treaty instead. Borah and Morrison at this time viewed a two-party treaty as unhelpful to Outlawry.

Then there is a June 24th letter from Levinson with recommendations and a draft treaty. Kellogg had asked Levinson to send him a draft. What Levinson produced was a bilateral treaty containing six short articles. The first committed the two nations to never using war or force in any form to settle disputes between them. This did not prevent their using force against other nations. The second article asserted the claims of the Monroe Doctrine, namely that the United States was committed to intervening should a European nation assert any power in the

Americas. Article III renounced war between the United States and France. Article IV allowed self-defense. Article V committed the two nations to settling disputes between them through an "arbitral or judicial tribunal." And Article VI essentially repeated Article V. Here was a draft treaty created not by a corrupt and compromising government official but by the originator of this moral crusade, and it was not nearly as strong as the final Kellogg-Briand Pact would be.

Scrolling down a bit in Kellogg's papers on microfilm is a letter from Levinson on June 27, 1927, that reads:

Dear Mr. Secretary:
I enclose the following Outlawry pamphlets:
1-Outlawry of War: What It Is and Is Not.
2-If War Were Outlawed.
3-Why Not Outlaw War?
By John Dewey

4-Public Opinion Outlaws War.
5-Outlawry of War!
By Hon. Wm. E. Borah

6-Can Peace Be Enforced?
7-The Prevention of War!
8-Can War Be Outlawed?
9-The Draft Treaty and the Outlawry of War.
10-The Case in a Nutshell.
By the writer.

I saw Senator Borah yesterday and was delighted to know of your good interview and the prospects of harmonious action with reference to the Franco-American proposal. I took the liberty of giving him copy of the paper I sent you. On reading it he seemed to approve it highly. I discussed the matter at length with him and he is pretty generally in accord with the ideas expressed in my letter to you.

Aside from the humanitarian aspect of this matter, it has great political potentialities. After the frictional differences created by the contest over the League and the Court, a simple clean-cut position against war would re-dedicate the great Republican Party as the party of abolition.

Sincerely yours,
S.O. Levinson

That same day, Kellogg wrote to President Coolidge sharing these ideas. If Coolidge and Kellogg were to get this done, it would have to be in the coming year-and-a-half, because on August 3rd Coolidge announced that he would not run for reelection in 1928. Among the names widely discussed as potential candidates to replace Coolidge was William Borah.

As the summer dragged on, Levinson paid Harrison Brown to promote Outlawry in Europe. His task was made more difficult when the state of Massachusetts killed Italian-American immigrants Ferdinanda Nicola Sacco and Bartolomeo Vanzetti on August 23rd, following what was widely viewed as an unfair trial for murder. That Senator Borah had offered his services to Sacco and Vanzetti was of some benefit. When Morrison's book was published, Brown was paid to hand it out. The book, *The Outlawry of War*, was the product of years of work. It included an addendum on the Briand proposal, edited at Levinson's strong urging to blame any shortcomings therein on Shotwell rather than on Briand.

On September 24, 1927, the League of Nations passed what came to be called the Polish resolution. It stated,

> 1-*That all wars of aggression are, and always shall be, prohibited.*
> 2-*That every pacific means must be employed to settle disputes, of every description, which may arise between states.*

Meanwhile, Kellogg encouraged President Coolidge to enlarge the U.S. Navy with the largest military spending bill since the World War. The Disarmament Conference failure turned Coolidge and Kellogg away from Europe. In September Kellogg finally met with French Ambassador Paul Louis Charles Claudel and told him he'd be unable to discuss the matter of a treaty against war until at least October.

CAPPER COMES THROUGH

When nothing more had progressed by November, Senator Arthur Capper of Kansas took it upon himself to act. Butler gave him a resolution shaped by Shotwell and Chamberlain. Capper sought Levinson's advice as well, but rejected Levinson's preference for deleting a paragraph that defined aggressive war. Capper gave his resolution to the press on November 21, 1927. This development suggested to the nation that the farmers of the Midwest were behind Briand's proposal, or at least not against it. The *Pocatello Tribune* arrived at this cynical interpretation:

> *The real significance of the Capper plan to withhold support from any citizen who deals with an aggressor in war lies in its showing the belief of western politicians that the voters who prevented American entry into the league are aware that if Europe spends a disproportionate share of its limited funds in military preparation it will have little left for American wheat and corn.*

This was, of course, before the weapons exporters came to hold more sway in Washington than the wheat and corn exporters.

In the "whereas" clauses of the resolution, Capper cited the August 29, 1916, Congressional statement against the use of war quoted above. He quoted from Briand's April 6, 1927, proposal. He pointed to strong public support, noted that the arbitration treaty with France would expire on February 27, 1928, and foreswore any national obligation to protect U.S. citizens who engage in hostilities abroad. Then his resolution declared it the policy of the United States,

I. By treaty with France and other like-minded nations formally to renounce war as an instrument of public policy and to adjust and settle its international disputes by mediation, arbitration and conciliation; and

II. By formal declaration to accept the definition of aggressor nation as one which, having agreed to submit international differences to conciliation, arbitration or judicial settlement, begins hostilities without having done so; and

III. By treaty with France and other like-minded nations to declare that the nationals of the contracting governments should not be protected by their governments in giving aid and comfort to an aggressor nation; and

Be it further resolved, That the President be requested to enter into negotiations with France and other like-minded nations for the purpose of concluding treaties with such nations, in furtherance of the declared policy of the United States.

Capper told the press "If M. Briand's proposal be accepted as between the United States and France and offers are made to extend it to Great Britain, to Germany, to Japan and to Italy, the chance of future wars would be reduced to a minimum so long as other contracting nations keep the faith. As it is obvious that they themselves would not go to war with each other and by refusing jointly and severally to aid an aggressor nation, they would thereby make any war between two lesser nations virtually a local affair. . . . Within the next year, in February, June, and August the treaties of arbitration with France, Great Britain and Japan expire by their own terms. The adoption of this resolution opens the way for treaties in their place renouncing war between these important nations. Here is a vital matter. We have here a great opportunity to live up to our highest American traditions in this resolution to renounce war. We should make the most of it."

Charles DeBenedetti, in a 1972 article titled "Borah and the Kellogg-Briand Pact," gives a great deal of credit to the Capper resolution. He thinks the combination of a number of Republican leaders backing former Secretary of State Charles Evans Hughes for the Republican presidential nomination and Capper's introducing a resolution coming out of the Butler-Shotwell camp led Borah to swing behind the Briand offer and "manipulate it toward his own ends." In DeBenedetti's view, those ends were extremely undesirable, amounting to marking the treaty with "purposelessness," by stripping it of entanglements and alliances. In an alternative interpretation, through Borah's adoption of this campaign the nations involved ended up banning all war in order to (1) avoid banning only aggressive war, and (2) avoid doing nothing. Without the peace movement's pressure, the U.S. government would have done nothing at all.

In late 1927 support for the Capper resolution came from the Federal Council of Churches of Christ in America, the American Branch of the World Alliance for International Friendship Through the Churches, and women's groups led by Carrie Chapman Catt. Representatives Theodore Burton (Republican, Ohio) and Hamilton Fish Jr. (Republican, New York) soon announced that they would introduce resolutions like Capper's.

BRINGING IN BORAH
AND KELLOGG

B orah got involved after relentless lobbying by Levinson, lobbying that included making Borah a trustee of the American Committee for the Outlawry of War; sending him several thousand dollars, mostly used for reprinting speeches; sending Borah's wife an amber necklace and a radio; and trying to send Borah more money and an automobile which he refused.

Borah drafted an Outlawry resolution for the National Grange that was endorsed by its 800,000 members. On November 10, 1927, Borah publicly proposed including Great Britain, Japan, Germany, and Italy in a treaty outlawing war.

Borah came around to supporting the Kellogg-Briand Pact by way of opposing what Briand had initially suggested. On November 26, 1927, Borah wrote in the *New York Times*: "I do not think peace plans which turn upon the question of an 'aggressor nation' are workable. An aggressor nation is a delusive and wholly impracticable proposition as a factor in any peace plan." Shotwell considered an aggressor a nation that failed to submit to arbitration before resorting to war. Borah believed a nation could draft an ultimatum that would lead its victim to reject arbitration. "I would not support a peace plan which recognized war as legitimate at any time or under any circumstances," he wrote.

Yet, from November on, Borah worked hard to get a treaty — a universal treaty — passed. Borah avoided his usual approach of publicly attacking Coolidge and Kellogg. Instead he chose to privately tutor them in Outlawry and publicly encourage them gently. Borah even showed great restraint in his statements about the French as negotiations proceeded.

One little possible glitch was that President Coolidge believed that outlawing war was probably unconstitutional. He said as much publicly on November 25th. In his December 6, 1927, State of the Union address, Coolidge remarked: "We should continue to promote peace by our example, and fortify it by such international covenants as we are permitted under our Constitution to make."

The argument for the unconstitutionality of outlawing war was ultimately refuted by the Ring Lardner method ("Shut up, he explained.") Coolidge could not resist the public demand for peace, and there was no popular movement behind the claim for unconstitutionality. But the argument was susceptible to refutation by legal reasoning as well. The argument was essentially that the Congress had been given the power to declare war by Article I of the Constitution. This power has since been erased by numerous presidents launching and escalating wars on their own and telling Congress to go jump in a lake. But here the claim was that Congress could not be deprived of its power to decide matters of war through a treaty banning all war.

This idea was refuted in 1927 by the following reasoning: Such a restriction on treaty making would effectively ban the making of any treaties, since Congress constitutionally holds power over all the areas that treaties address. Congress had the power to "raise and support armies" but Congress had ratified disarmament treaties, and Coolidge was working to create more. Congress had the power "to regulate commerce with foreign nations," but Congress had also ratified tariff agreements. Congress had the power to grant "letters of marque and reprisal," that is, to license pirates, a practice that had effectively been banned and outmoded. The ideal of an eternal Constitution alterable only by amendment is often forced aside by cultural changes. And Congress had been given the power to declare war, not in order to ensure that we had enough wars, but in order to deprive the executive of that power. The U.S. president would remain in exactly the same constitutional position if war were outlawed, namely lacking any right to make war.

Meanwhile the Soviet Union's delegate to the Preparatory Commission for Disarmament made an interesting proposal on November 30, 1927. He proposed immediate and total abolition of all armies, navies, and air forces; the sinking of all warships; the scrapping of all war material; and the demolition of all arms factories. Maxim Maximovich Litvinov (1876-1951) would go on to struggle for years to build better relations between the Soviet Union and western nations, and to warn western nations against their support for Nazism in Germany. But the governments of Europe and the United States simply rejected his proposal for disarmament. A few weeks later, the French Chamber of Deputies voted 150 million francs to enlarge France's navy.

Briand's proposed treaty was kept secret by both Briand and Kellogg. On December 7, 1927, Representative Hamilton Fish Jr.

introduced a resolution asking Kellogg to provide Congress with Briand's proposal. Kellogg refused to do so.

On December 10, 1927, French Ambassador Claudel met with Assistant Secretary of State Castle and proposed to drop the idea of a new treaty and to just combine all recent proposals into a renewal of the Franco-American treaty of arbitration — the Root treaty. Claudel said that he knew the U.S. Senate would not agree to a treaty of general arbitration. He thought the public could be satisfied by a strong preamble introducing what some people would call a weak treaty, namely a reproduction of the existing treaty. (The preambles or "whereas" clauses of treaties are often considered nonbinding by those preferring not to be bound by them. Yet they often answer to public sentiment and serve to appease the demands of people who are unaware that their legislators have their fingers crossed behind their backs.)

Claudel and Castle agreed to renounce war in a preamble. And they did so in an arbitration treaty with France that would be signed by Undersecretary of State Robert Olds in Kellogg's absence on February 6, 1928. The same preamble language would make it into other Kellogg arbitration treaties.

Also on December 10, 1927, Jane Addams led a delegation to the White House and delivered a petition with 30,000 names. Coolidge assured her that he would try to achieve the treaty with France. Addams sent the same petition to Briand who thanked her.

On December 12th, Borah introduced his resolution on Outlawry for the fourth time. On December 14th, Kellogg said he supported Capper's plan to end aggressive war. Borah denounced the idea of "aggressive war" and worked on bringing Kellogg around.

Claudel again met with Castle and proposed that Foreign Minister Briand come to the United States to sign a treaty outlawing war. Castle thought that Briand was simply trying to add Washington to "the halo of Locarno," in order to benefit himself politically. Castle told Claudel that an Outlawry treaty would take away Congress' power to declare war and would be "playing into the hands of the pacifists."

The Senate Foreign Relations Committee held a closed meeting on December 21, 1927, at which Kellogg discussed the arbitration treaty, and Borah told him:

"But, Mr. Secretary, all this does not dispose of the proposal to outlaw war."

Kellogg claimed it did.

Borah — according to an account that probably came from Borah — proposed extending a treaty to include all the nations of the world. Borah polled the senators and found them supportive or noncommittal. "I think, Mr. Secretary, you may consider it the sense of this committee," Borah concluded, "that you go ahead with the negotiation of a pact to include all countries."

Kellogg later disputed this account and claimed that the idea, in fact, had originated with him. In reality, as we've seen, the idea had been in Borah's public statements for months and was in line with the demands of the public movement for Outlawry, but it was also true that rumors had been floated for months that the State Department could only act multilaterally, rumors probably coming from Kellogg's assistants. The idea was in Marriner's memo as well.

Borah persuaded Kellogg to back a multilateral treaty, and Kellogg persuaded Borah to back renewal of the 1908 arbitration treaty. Out of this bargain, Borah's political prospects brightened as the chance of a treaty fitting Capper's resolution ever seeing the light of day diminished.

On December 23, 1927, Kellogg laid out the idea of a multilateral Outlawry treaty to Elihu Root concluding, "You know, of course, that there is tremendous demand in this country and probably in foreign countries for the so-called outlawry of war. Nobody knows just what that means . . . . I think this would answer."

Briand sent a Christmas message directly to the American people, not to their Secretary of State or their President, in which he stressed the dangers of conflict breaking out in Eastern Europe and the need for U.S. involvement in the work of making peace.

Come December 28th, Kellogg had finally prepared a response to Briand as well as a counterproposal creating a multilateral treaty. He was hesitating to send it, however. When Kellogg learned that he would be receiving a note from Briand at 4 p.m., he quickly obtained President Coolidge's authorization and sent his note off to Briand. The note expected from Briand at 4 p.m. was never delivered. Kellogg had beaten him to the draw, if that's the appropriate metaphor. Two days later Claudel called on Kellogg. Claudel still wanted a bilateral agreement.

Carrie Chapman Catt

CARRIE CHAPMAN CATT

Carrie Chapman Catt was born in Ripon, Wisconsin, in 1859, five years after the Republican Party had been born there. Her family moved to Iowa when she was seven. She worked her way through college and was a teacher until she married. Married women were forbidden to teach. She wrote a newspaper column on women's politics, and when her husband died she took up freelance work in San Francisco at the age of 27. There she met George Catt, whom she would marry in 1890, but in the meantime, she became a public lecturer and returned to Iowa in 1887.

In Iowa, Carrie Chapman joined the Women's Christian Temperance Union and became head of its suffrage section. In 1889 she was elected secretary of the Iowa Woman Suffrage Association. In 1890 she was a delegate and speaker at the National American Woman Suffrage Association (NAWSA) conference. Married that year, Carrie Chapman Catt traveled the country organizing for women's suffrage, including in Colorado, where in 1893 the men of Colorado voted to allow women to vote. Catt was often too exhausted or ill to travel and would use her rest time for writing.

In 1900, Susan B. Anthony retired and Catt was elected president of NAWSA. She founded the International Woman Suffrage Alliance in 1902 and was its president until 1923. But she resigned as president of NAWSA in 1904 for reasons of health, her own and her husband's. In 1911, she toured the world, founding women's suffrage organizations in Europe, Asia, and Africa. By this time, Idaho, Washington, and California had voted for suffrage, as did additional states including New York in 1917.

In 1915, Catt again became president of NAWSA, but she was torn between the suffrage movement and the cause of world peace. Also in 1915, she helped establish the Woman's Peace Party. In 1914 Catt had been left $2 million in a will with the intention that it be used to win suffrage. After legal battles with the donor's family members, Catt retained $977,875, which she used as intended, breathing dramatic new life into the movement.

Catt believed that women's suffrage would help the cause of peace, but she was willing to sacrifice the cause of peace to get it. She announced NAWSA's support for President Wilson and entry into World War I. In March 1919, with the war over and victory of suffrage near, she established the League of Women Voters as NAWSA's successor. In 1920, the 36th state ratified the Nineteenth Amendment, and the cause was won.

What to do now?

Catt now devoted herself to peace, campaigning for American membership in the League of Nations. In 1925, she helped to create the Committee on the Cause and Cure of War, and she would serve as its chair until 1932. It very quickly gathered five million members and became a force in lobbying for the Kellogg-Briand Pact.

In January 1928, the Committee on the Cause and Cure of War held its third annual conference in Washington, D.C. Secretary of War Dwight F. Davis, Admiral Frank H. Schofield, and Assistant Secretary of State William R. Castle spoke at the conference, all claiming that the United States was more opposed to war than any other nation. The conference passed a resolution backing the Kellogg proposal for a multilateral treaty renouncing war. One delegate, Annie Matthews, opposed the measure, declaring Kellogg to be insincere and not a true believer in peace. That wasn't exactly the point. If we only approve of steps toward peace taken by true believers, we may as well give up the idea of imposing peace on politicians. If Matthews had refused to work with anyone who had ever supported war, she would have had to refuse to work with Catt herself and many others present.

THE WORLD MAKES PEACE

Aristide Briand wrote to Frank Kellogg on January 5, 1928. He now proposed that France and the United States sign a treaty first and then allow others to sign it. But he still wanted to renounce "wars of aggression." Kellogg and Castle rejected this idea. Claudel argued that outlawing all war was "sentimental" and would please "bolshevists and socialists and cranks of all varieties." He suggested that some wars were good, such as then-current U.S. war making in Nicaragua. He may have been unaware of the immunity of U.S. politicians' brains to charges of hypocrisy. And it would appear that France was reluctant to ban all war because it envisioned making use of war in the future. Claudel proposed a joint declaration of principles instead of a treaty.

The trouble with that was that Kellogg wanted a treaty now.

On January 11, 1928, Kellogg wrote to Briand again proposing a universal treaty renouncing all war. Kellogg also made public what Briand's secret proposal had been. The Havana International Conference of American States was underway, and the French press was denouncing U.S. imperialism. On January 21st, Briand replied again, wanting again a bilateral treaty and a ban on aggression. Briand trumpeted the strong preamble to the arbitration treaty, but the State Department pointed out that it was nonbinding. This was beginning to look like a stalemate. Game over. Thank you, one and all, for playing.

And then somebody made another move from the far side of the board. On February 5th, Senator Borah published a front-page article in the *New York Times Magazine*, an article prepared largely by Levinson. The headline was "One Great Treaty to Outlaw All Wars." Borah claimed that a breach of the treaty by one nation would release other nations from complying with it in relation to that violator. This would allow self-defense. It would also allow France to sign such a treaty while still upholding its treaties forming alliances to respond to war. This idea had already been proposed by Claudel, and prior to that by Shotwell, yet it seemed to be a sticking point for the professional diplomats.

On February 27, 1928, Kellogg sent a third note to Briand similar to the previous two. Kellogg, in Ferrell's analysis, had now accomplished two goals: appeasing the peace movement and discomfiting Briand. But now "he began to believe that a multilateral treaty really would be a great gift to the world." And he was planning to retire on March 4, 1929. Castle wrote in his diary that their efforts had "appealed enormously to the Pacifists and the Earnest Christians but . . . I think it is about time for the correspondence to stop. The political trick has been turned and now we should take a well deserved rest. The funny thing is that Olds and the Secretary seem to take it all with profound seriousness. . . ." Castle, heir to U.S. exploitation of Hawaii, couldn't believe his boss had gone over to the side of the "_____ _____ pacifists." Levinson was disappointed that Kellogg was not using the term "outlaw," but he praised the Secretary and wrote to him on February 29th "The Nobel Peace Prize should be yours."

Kellogg was now on board both with publicly banning war and with using public negotiations to achieve that end. On March 15, 1928, the Secretary gave a public speech at the Council on Foreign Relations, in which he made his argument for the treaty. Kellogg began,

> It has been my privilege during the past few months to conduct on behalf of the Government of the United States negotiations having for their object the promotion of the great ideal of world peace. Popular and governmental interest in the realization of this ideal has never been greater than at the present time.

He cited a (nonbinding) resolution renouncing war as an instrument of national policy just signed by 17 members of the League of Nations at the Havana Inter-American Conference. If they could pretend to renounce all war, surely they could renounce it for real; clearly membership in the League of Nations did not prevent a nation from renouncing war as an instrument of policy — the same language, Kellogg noted, that Briand had proposed to him for a bilateral treaty — language that in fact could be traced back to the _____ _____ pacifists. In this speech, Kellogg made the Outlawrist argument against the possibility of defining and criminalizing aggression. Kellogg may or may not have fully grasped the moral vision of Outlawry and the paradigm change that Morrison and Levinson had in mind for international relations, but he sure as heck understood what kind of treaty could survive a ratification vote in William Borah's Senate.

In Kellogg's papers are letters to Kellogg praising his speech, and thank-you notes back from him. Levinson asked for and was sent 25 copies of the transcript. The text of Kellogg's speeches and much of Kellogg's correspondence with France, including draft treaties, can also be found in James Thayer Gerould's 1929 book *Selected Articles on the Pact of Paris: Officially the General Pact for the Renunciation of War.*

In March 1928, Claudel again tried to get Olds to support a declaration of principles instead of a treaty, but Olds certainly knew Kellogg wouldn't go for that. Kellogg sent a letter to Herrick on March 19th asking that he hint to Briand that it would be wise to act while Kellogg remained in office.

That message seems to have hit the spot. On March 30th Briand replied, agreeing to Kellogg's proposed treaty as long as it was universal, as long as a breach would release its signers from compliance, and as long as self-defense would remain. Kellogg accepted all of these points, objecting only to strict universality, preferring that the treaty take effect even if some country or countries held out.

On April 13, 1928, Kellogg sent a draft treaty to Italy, Japan, Germany, and Great Britain. One week later, Briand sent those countries a draft of his own. Briand's version included reservations for self-defense, other treaty obligations, etc. While

Kellogg agreed with such reservations via correspondence, he did not want them written into the treaty or officially attached to it. He certainly did not want the treaty to include support for other treaties that involved alliances and the use of force. Kellogg considered what Briand had drafted to be a "justification rather than a renunciation of the use of armed force."

Kellogg gave a second public speech, this one to the American Society of International Law, on April 28th. In this speech, he established his official interpretation of what the Kellogg-Briand Pact would mean, an interpretation he shared with other nations but which was not made officially part of the treaty. In this manner Kellogg was able — whether he had this in mind at the time or not — to assure potential signatories that the treaty would leave them with the right to self-defense, and would free them of obligations if another signatory violated the pact, without allowing such reservations to mar the simplicity of the treaty itself.

In Europe some progress was slowly being made as well. Briand attended a meeting of the League of Nations in Geneva which ended up encouraging him to pursue the treaty. French, British, and German diplomats met secretly to discuss it. In Britain, Secretary of State for Foreign Affairs Austen Chamberlain, defending his delays to the Parliament and the press, claimed that Great Britain "has never treated war as an instrument of national policy." His opponents pointed to the South African War (the Boer Wars), and Chamberlain said he would not "go back to ancient history and the Crusaders." Shotwell commented on this: "it apparently seemed to the son of Joseph Chamberlain that centuries had intervened since the day of Britain's last great imperial adventure . . . and yet hardly a generation had intervened." Joseph Chamberlain (1836-1914), Austen's father, had been Secretary of State for the Colonies at the turn of the century when the British had used concentration camps to eliminate large numbers of people in South Africa.

The House of Lords passed a resolution backing the American proposal "whilst recognizing the desire of His Majesty's Government to cooperate in securing the peace of the world." On May 19, 1928, Britain sent the United States a note that expressed concern over British imperial interests, paralleling U.S. concern over the Monroe Doctrine. Both nations' governments viewed their imperialism as falling into the category of self-defense. Chamberlain's statement came to be known in the press as the "British Monroe Doctrine." Levinson and the Outlawrists lobbied Britain hard against pressing this as a formal reservation to the treaty.

U.S. Senator John Blaine, a Republican from Wisconsin, remarked in the Senate in 1928: "We have turned the Monroe Doctrine into an agency of mischief for America, not for her protection or the protection of weaker nations and peoples (but as an instrument that made American intervention), the wet nurse for alien governments, money lenders, adventurers, and concession-grabbers in their career of expansion, extension, and exploitation."

Monroe Doctrine or not, a movement to outlaw war was hitting its stride. The Women's International League for Peace and Freedom passed a resolution commending Kellogg on May 5, 1928.

So did the American Peace Society. The National Committee on the Cause and Cure of War's 12 million women planned 48 state conferences through which to influence the Senate when it came time to ratify a treaty renouncing war.

On June 23rd, Kellogg sent 14 countries the text of his proposed treaty and the U.S. interpretation thereof. Germany formally agreed on July 11th, as did France three days later, followed by Italy:

> *I hardly need assure you that Italy, adhering to the policy which she is constantly following, has welcomed with lively sympathy this initiative and offers very willingly her cordial collaboration toward reaching an agreement.*

Thus spoke Italian Minister of Foreign Affairs Benito Mussolini to U.S. Ambassador Henry Fletcher. Conceivably Mussolini wasn't speaking from his deepest being with complete sincerity.

Japan, despite its outrage over the U.S. "Japanese Exclusion Bill," agreed to the Kellogg-Briand Pact. Japan raised no concerns or reservations, despite having developed its own U.S.-approved Monroe Doctrine for Asia (read James Bradley's 2009 book *The Imperial Cruise*), and despite the potential for conflict in Manchuria.

In the end, agreeing to sign the pact by July 20th would be Australia, Belgium, Canada, Czechoslovakia, France, Germany, India, the Irish Free State, Italy, Japan, New Zealand, Poland, South Africa, the United Kingdom, and the United States. And these additional nations would sign on to adhere to it: Afghanistan,

Albania, Austria, Bulgaria, China, Cuba, Denmark, Dominican Republic, Egypt, Estonia, Ethiopia, Finland, Guatemala, Hungary, Iceland, Latvia, Liberia, Lithuania, the Netherlands, Nicaragua, Norway, Panama, Peru, Portugal, Romania, the Soviet Union, the Kingdom of the Serbs, Croats, and Slovenes, Siam, Spain, Sweden, and Turkey. Eight further states joined after that date: Persia, Greece, Honduras, Chile, Luxembourg, Danzig, Costa Rica, and Venezuela.

Extra points if you know what Persia is called today!

The U.S. State Department lists the treaty as still in force with these current nations as parties, some of them having joined relatively recently: Afghanistan, Albania, Antigua & Barbuda, Australia, Austria, Barbados, Belgium, Bosnia-Herzegovina, Brazil, Bulgaria, Canada, Chile, Colombia, Costa Rica, Cuba, Czech Republic, Denmark, Dominica, Dominican Republic, Ecuador, Egypt, Estonia, Ethiopia, Fiji, Finland, France, Germany, Greece, Guatemala, Haiti, Honduras, Hungary, Iceland, India, Iran, Iraq, Ireland, Italy, Japan, Latvia, Liberia, Lithuania, Luxembourg, Mexico, Netherlands, New Zealand, Nicaragua, Norway, Panama, Paraguay, Peru, Poland, Portugal, Romania, Saudi Arabia, Slovenia, South Africa, Spain, Sweden, Switzerland, Taiwan, Thailand, Turkey, former members of the Union of Soviet Socialist Republics, United Kingdom, United States, Venezuela.

The Kellogg-Briand Pact was put together in an extremely public manner, and as these things go it was agreed to very quickly and with an unusually high number of adhering nations. Most observers give public opinion and public pressure the credit. The U.S. peace movement was fully behind it, and that unity was a new and powerful force. About the public opinion in favor of the Peace Pact it is worth noting a couple of things. First, the propaganda campaign that had brought public opinion around to supporting war in 1917 had been far more extensive, vastly more expensive, and backed up by a police force. The peace movement did not have to intimidate or lie to anyone in the United States to gain their support for Kellogg-Briand. Secondly, the same was true with foreign heads of state acting in accordance with the wishes of their peoples: Unlike the formation of a coalition of nations to invade Iraq in 2003, this coalition of nations to outlaw war was put together without bribery or threats being required.

Kellogg signs the Kellogg-Briand Pact.

THE STRANGEST DREAM

Kellogg proposed that the signing of the pact take place not in Washington, but in Paris. He proposed to take part himself. For the signing, Paris' government buildings flew the flags of Germany, the Soviet Union, and all the other nations. This is what was signed on August 27, 1928:

THE PRESIDENT OF THE GERMAN REICH, THE PRESIDENT OF THE UNITED STATES OF AMERICA, HIS MAJESTY THE KING OF THE BELGIANS, THE PRESIDENT OF THE FRENCH REPUBLIC, HIS MAJESTY THE KING OF GREAT BRITAIN IRELAND AND THE BRITISH DOMINIONS BEYOND THE SEAS, EMPEROR OF INDIA, HIS MAJESTY THE KING OF ITALY, HIS MAJESTY THE EMPEROR OF JAPAN, THE PRESIDENT OF THE REPUBLIC OF POLAND, THE PRESIDENT OF THE CZECHOSLOVAK REPUBLIC,

Deeply sensible of their solemn duty to promote the welfare of mankind;

Persuaded that the time has, come when a frank renunciation of war as an instrument of national policy should be made to the end that the peaceful and friendly relations now existing between their peoples may be perpetuated;

Convinced that all changes in their relations with one another should be sought only by pacific means and be the result of a peaceful and orderly process, and that any signatory Power which shall hereafter seek to promote its national interests by resort to war a should be denied the benefits furnished by this Treaty;

Hopeful that, encouraged by their example, all the other nations of the world will join in this humane endeavor and by adhering to the present Treaty as soon as it comes into force bring their peoples within the scope of its beneficent provisions, thus uniting the civilized nations of the world in a common renunciation of war as an instrument of their national policy;

Have decided to conclude a Treaty and for that purpose have appointed as their respective Plenipotentiaries:

THE PRESIDENT OF THE GERMAN REICH:
Dr Gustav STRESEMANN, Minister of Foreign Affairs;

THE PRESIDENT OF THE UNITED STATES OF AMERICA:
The Honorable Frank B. KELLOGG, Secretary of State;

HIS MAJESTY THE KING OF THE BELGIANS:
Mr. Paul HYMANS, Minister for Foreign Affairs, Minister of State;

THE PRESIDENT OF THE FRENCH REPUBLIC:
Mr. Aristide BRIAND Minister for Foreign Affairs;

HIS MAJESTY THE KING OF GREAT BRITAIN,
IRELAND AND THE BRITISH DOMINIONS BEYOND
THE SEAS, EMPEROR OF INDIA:

For GREAT BRITAIN and NORTHERN IRELAND and all
parts of the British Empire which are not separate Members
of the League of Nations:
The Right Honourable Lord CUSHENDUN, Chancellor
of the Duchy of Lancaster, Acting-Secretary of State for
Foreign Affairs;

For the DOMINION OF CANADA:
The Right Honourable William Lyon MACKENZIE KING,
Prime Minister and Minister for External Affairs;

For the COMMONWEALTH of AUSTRALIA:
The Honourable Alexander John McLACHLAN, Member of
the Executive Federal Council;

For the DOMINION OF NEW ZEALAND:
The Honourable Sir Christopher James PARR High
Commissioner for New Zealand in Great Britain;

For the UNION OF SOUTH AFRICA:
The Honourable Jacobus Stephanus SMIT, High Comm-
issioner for the Union of South Africa in Great Britain;

For the IRISH FREE STATE:
Mr. William Thomas COSGRAVE, President of the Executive Council;

For INDIA:
The Right Honourable Lord CUSHENDUN, Chancellor of the Duchy of Lancaster, Acting Secretary of State for Foreign Affairs;

HIS MAJESTY THE KING OF ITALY:
Count Gaetano MANZONI, his Ambassador Extraordinary and Plenipotentiary at Paris;

HIS MAJESTY THE EMPEROR OF JAPAN:
Count UCHIDA, Privy Councillor;

THE PRESIDENT OF THE REPUBLIC OF POLAND:
Mr. A. ZALESKI, Minister for Foreign Affairs;

THE PRESIDENT OF THE CZECHOSLOVAK REPUBLIC:
Dr Eduard BENES, Minister for Foreign Affairs;

who, having communicated to one another their full powers found in good and due form have agreed upon the following articles:

ARTICLE I
The High Contracting Parties solemnly declare in the names of their respective peoples that they condemn recourse to war

for the solution of international controversies, and renounce it, as an instrument of national policy in their relations with one another.

ARTICLE II

The High Contracting Parties agree that the settlement or solution of all disputes or conflicts of whatever nature or of whatever origin they may be, which may arise among them, shall never be sought except by pacific means.

ARTICLE III

The present Treaty shall be ratified by the High Contracting Parties named in the Preamble in accordance with their respective constitutional requirements, and shall take effect as between them as soon as all their several instruments of ratification shall have been deposited at Washington.

This Treaty shall, when it has come into effect as prescribed in the preceding paragraph, remain open as long as may be necessary for adherence by all the other Powers of the world. Every instrument evidencing the adherence of a Power shall be deposited at Washington and the Treaty shall immediately upon such deposit become effective as; between the Power thus adhering and the other Powers parties hereto.

It shall be the duty of the Government of the United States to furnish each Government named in the Preamble and every Government subsequently adhering to this Treaty with a certified copy of the Treaty and of every instrument of ratification or adherence. It shall also be the duty of the Government of the United States telegraphically to notify such Governments immediately upon the deposit with it of each instrument of ratification or adherence.

IN FAITH WHEREOF the respective Plenipotentiaries have signed this Treaty in the French and English languages both texts having equal force, and hereunto affix their seals.

DONE at Paris, the twenty seventh day of August in the year one thousand nine hundred and twenty-eight.

[SEAL] GUSTAV STRESEMANN
[SEAL] FRANK B KELLOGG
[SEAL] PAUL HYMANS
[SEAL] ARI BRIAND
[SEAL] CUSHENDUN
[SEAL] W. L. MACKENZIE KING
[SEAL] A J MCLACHLAN
[SEAL] C. J. PARR
[SEAL] J S. SMIT
[SEAL] LIAM T. MACCOSGAIR
[SEAL] CUSHENDUN
[SEAL] G. MANZONI
[SEAL] UCHIDA
[SEAL] AUGUST ZALESKI
[SEAL] DR EDWARD BENES

In Aristide Briand's speech that day, he noted that for the first time in over half a century a representative of France was receiving a German Foreign Minister on French soil. Briand also said, as quoted above,

> *For the first time, on a scale as absolute as it is vast, a treaty has been truly devoted to the very establishment of peace, and has laid down laws that are new and free from all political considerations. Such a treaty means a beginning and not an end.*

Robert Underwood Johnson, a U.S. writer and diplomat, wrote of the occasion:

> *Lift up your heads, ye peoples,*
> *The miracle has come.*
> *No longer are ye helpless,*
> *No longer are ye dumb.*

But Ambassador Herrick wrote to a colleague on the occasion that he didn't think peace would actually arrive for perhaps 100 or 500 years yet.

This was the strangest dream: "I dreamed I saw a mighty room, and the room was filled with men." And it truly was filled with men. The Inter-American Commission of Women and other U.S. and British feminists picketed the signing ceremony, demanding to present an equal rights treaty to the international delegates and facing arrest and police abuse as a result. The dream still needed perfecting, to say the least. The dream also needed ratifying by the U.S. Senate, and in that struggle countless feminists would lead the way in supporting the treaty.

When Frank Kellogg had boarded a ship in New York on August 18, 1928, to sail to the signing ceremony in Paris, he had been protested by 100 members of the Anti-Imperialist League with signs reading "Hands Off Nicaragua," "Down With American Imperialism," and "Down With Kellogg's Fake Peace Treaty." Had I been alive at the time, I would have been with them. Being alive now, I celebrate the treaty. Those who push harder for higher goals contribute as much as anyone else to those accomplishments that are realized. And those pushing were not confined to the New York docks. Senator La Follette, among others, was advocating a three-point plan of Outlawry, disarmament, and withdrawal from Nicaragua.

While in Paris, Kellogg knelt at the tomb of the Unknown Soldier, under the Arc de Triomphe.

While Kellogg was aboard a ship home from France, Herbert Hoover claimed the Kellogg-Briand Pact as an achievement of the Republican Party. Kellogg, not knowing this, was asked on arrival whether the Pact should be part of political campaigns or nonpartisan. He maintained that it should be the latter. In fact, support for the Kellogg-Briand Pact was made part of both the Republican and Democratic Party Platforms in 1928. However, in his speech nominating Alfred E. Smith (Alfred E. who?) for president, a leading Democrat took the opportunity to belittle the Kellogg-Briand Pact. He would later find the opportunity to violate it. His name was Franklin Delano Roosevelt.

As you may have guessed, Hoover defeated Smith in the 1928 presidential election, in which peace advocate Norman Thomas was the Socialist candidate. After the election, the peace movement pushed hard for ratification, led by Carrie Chapman Catt's Committee on the Cause and Cure of War, the World Peace Foundation, the Carnegie Endowment for International Peace, the American Committee for the Outlawry of War, the Commission on International Justice and Goodwill of the Federal Council of Churches of Christ in America, the World Alliance for International Friendship, plus all kinds of churches and women's clubs. Resolutions, telegrams, and letters flooded the senators. The Committee on the Cause and Cure of War held over 10,000 meetings around the country and carefully whipped every senator. Catt said, "We are convinced from our experience of the past six months that the women of this Nation are more united in their endorsement of this treaty than we have ever known them to be on any other question." She may have meant to include even the question of suffrage in that claim.

On Armistice Day, November 11, 1928, Secretary Kellogg spoke in New York City, his speech followed by a two-day "Goodwill Congress" conference which included Senator Borah speaking at Carnegie Hall on Nov. 13th. Also on Armistice Day, in contrast, President Coolidge proposed more ships for the Navy.

On November 27, 1928, Senator Claude Swanson of Virginia,

the ranking Democrat on Foreign Relations (and no relation to this author) publicly backed the Kellogg-Briand Pact.

The peace movement was expanding more rapidly than ever. New organizations were formed overnight. Staff were hired; letters mailed; speakers bureaus established and put to work; and weekly mailings made to ministers, editors, and college student groups. On December 1, 1928, Kellogg sent Borah a list of organizations that had passed resolutions in favor of the Pact. The State Department had not received a single petition against it. On December 3rd, President Coolidge praised the Kellogg-Briand Pact in his State of the Union address.

However, militarists, including Coolidge, were pushing a bill for more Navy cruisers, competing for time on the Senate floor with the necessary debate and vote on the Kellogg-Briand Pact. Borah was working to reduce the naval funding from $800,000 to $274,000, and to bring the Peace Pact to the floor — and to do so without formal reservations attached to it. Eventually agreement was reached to address both bills on January 3rd. Three days into the new year, the Senate would vote on whether to renounce war and on whether to build more weapons.

Briand signs the Kellogg-Briand Pact.

SURVIVING THE SENATE

L ong before Frank Kellogg returned from France, Thomas Jefferson returned from his sojourn there. Jefferson confronted George Washington, wanting to know why the constitutional convention had added a Senate to the plan, which had included only the single House when Jefferson had departed. Washington supposedly replied: "Why did you pour that coffee into your saucer?" Jefferson said, "To cool it." And Washington remarked, "Even so. We pour our legislation into the senatorial saucer to cool it." Heat, in this context, was understood as popular will. The Senate was created as an antidemocratic measure. Senators would not be elected, would not represent small districts but whole states, and would serve terms three times as long as those of Representatives.

Ever since, and even with the popular election of senators having been added in 1913, the Senate has been the hurdle for all things good and just. The House of Representatives, the President, foreign nations, U.S. states and cities — these are all relatively easy in comparison with getting something worthwhile through the U.S. Senate. The House tried to ban slavery, and the Senate refused. The House would later try to uphold civil rights, and the Senate would refuse. Any bill drafted in the House has to be made bad enough to survive the Senate if it is to be considered viable. The House Judiciary Committee refuses to impeach corrupt officials based on a prediction that the Senate will not convict them. No doubt the House could do a better job of ratifying treaties, but that role is assigned to the Senate by the Constitution. The Senate rejected membership in the League of Nations and the World Court. What would it do with a treaty renouncing all war?

Momentum in December 1928 was all in the right direction. On December 4th Kellogg wrote to Borah, noting that another 2,200 letters had just come in, making at least 50,000, with the daily rate on the rise. These were all in support of the Pact. That same day, Coolidge sent the treaty to the Senate for ratification.

Three days later, the Senate Foreign Relations Committee held its first hearing, at which Kellogg presented a case for public diplomacy and a disclaimer of any obligations arising from the treaty other than the obligation not to use war:

> *Any communications made with any of the governments up to the signing of the treaty have been published. I made up my mind when we started negotiations that the only way to obtain this treaty was to publish every note as it was delivered, and I do not think the treaty would ever have been signed if it had not been for the opinion of the world passing on these notes as they appeared, so that every country had full opportunity to discuss the treaty: and if they believed there were any obligations imposed on the United States beyond the agreement not to go to war, I think they would have suggested it. They knew, from the notes that I wrote, that I was not willing to impose any obligation on the United States. I knew that was out of the question. I*

knew that not many countries would agree to affirmative obligations, if we did.

A week later on December 14th, Senators James Reed and George Moses introduced a resolution proposing four reservations: no obligation of coercion, no effect on the Monroe doctrine, self-defense, and no entanglement with the League. Levinson and the Outlawrists lobbied hard against any such reservations. They did not object to the substance of these or some other reservations proposed, but they objected to attaching any of them to the treaty itself, its simplicity constituting a large part of its powerful appeal. Kellogg had to talk Senator Hiram Bingham out of pushing a reservation to allow the United States to make war to protect its citizens abroad.

Many senators openly criticized the Pact, some rejecting it as worthless. Senator William Bruce, a Democrat from Maryland, called the Kellogg-Briand Pact "about as effective to keep down war as a carpet would be to smother an earthquake, but which, nevertheless, has worked up all the unsophisticated humanitarians of both sexes to a high state of excitement." Bruce favored joining the Court and the League. He considered Outlawry far less serious as a means toward war prevention. And yet, he said that he would nonetheless vote in favor of it.

He didn't have much choice. Senators continued reading petitions into the Congressional Record. The Federal Council of Churches brought the White House a petition with 180,000 signatures. In this age before email, the letterboxes and telegrams were working at full capacity.

Come January, 3, 1929, Borah opened a debate on the floor of the full Senate. The debate did not go as smoothly as its outcome might suggest. Senator Reed interrupted to point out that the Spanish American War had been a fraud as far as any claim to self-defense, and that the Kellogg-Briand Pact would therefore have prevented it. Borah simply replied that if that were so, then yes the Pact would have prevented the war. Senator Henrik Shipstead, a Republican from Kellogg's state of Minnesota, later raised the same point with regard to the World War. Coolidge himself had claimed that the Pact could have prevented that war: "Had an agreement of this kind been in existence in 1914, there is every reason to suppose that it would have saved the situation and delivered the world from all the misery which was inflicted by the great war," Coolidge had remarked. Didn't every single nation involved claim self-defense, Shipstead asked. Borah admitted as much, and admitted that the treaty might not have prevented the war. Senator George McClean, a Republican from Connecticut, argued for disarmament instead of what he characterized as weak treaties.

A lot of senators offered a lot of sharp questioning, relatively free of the strict obedience to party leaders that has more recently been the norm. Senators' opinions ranged from believing passage would withdraw the United States from Nicaragua and China to believing the treaty meant nothing at all. Senator Carter Glass, a Democrat from Virginia, considered the Pact "worthless, but perfectly harmless." That was not, however, the common view across the country, as thousands of people worked night and day to promote passage.

In mid-January 1,000 women peace leaders from around the country lobbied their respective senators in Washington, delivering thousands of petitions. Carrie Chapman Catt, who led this effort, suffered a heart attack during it. Popular pressure was combined with pressure from those in power. President Coolidge persuaded Vice President Dawes to whip every senator to support the Pact.

On January 15th, Borah proposed and Dawes, Coolidge, and Kellogg agreed to pass the treaty plus a report from the Foreign Relations Committee as an interpretation of the treaty that would not formally be a modification or reservation to it. That day, the Senate voted 85 to 1 in favor of ratification, with nine senators not voting, and no reservations attached to the treaty.

Senator John Blaine of Wisconsin, the author of the 21st Amendment repealing prohibition, a strong opponent of wars and imperialism, but a Republican with a consistent habit of voting against any Republican proposals, was the unfortunate single "No" vote. The Wisconsin legislature passed a resolution censuring Blaine for his act of betrayal. Other senators who had expressed concerns all voted Yes. One explained his "Yes" vote by saying he did not want to be burned in effigy back in his state.

Two days after the vote, Coolidge signed the treaty into law. During the ceremony, ironically enough (and there is video of this), Coolidge lost his temper and shouted at a State Department employee who sought to help him "Who are you? I don't know you. Go away!" Kellogg later lost his own temper and cursed to Castle in recounting how the President had inexcusably lost *his* temper. Castle found this all very amusing in his diary.

Hoover declared the Pact in force on July 24, 1929.

The United States and Japan produced interpretive statements, not part of the treaty but nonetheless predictive of how those nations might behave. It also had taken Japan six months to sign the treaty because of these problematic words: "in the names of their respective peoples." The Japanese government had never done anything in the name of its people, but had always acted rather in the name of its emperor. France and Britain made reservations to the treaty.

Shotwell pointed out that the treaty did not use the term "outlaw" but rather "renounce," and that it renounced war as national (but not international) policy, meaning that a group of nations could still launch a war.

The idea that the whole world signed also requires some qualification. Signers and adherents, and the colonial territories and mandates occupied by signers or adherents, added up to most of the world. Of course, there is an enormous contradiction in this picture. Countries in Africa and elsewhere that were suppressed by war or the threat of war are thought of as having agreed to ban war, without any suggestion that the foreign occupations would therefore end.

And then there is a handful of countries that could not be said to have taken part in any way. The glaring exceptions to the Kellogg-Briand Pact were Mexico, El Salvador, Colombia, Ecuador, Brazil, Bolivia, Paraguay, Uruguay, and Argentina — in other words, much of the area targeted by the Monroe Doctrine. Mongolia, Nepal, San Marino, Yemen, and what is now Saudi Arabia were the only other exceptions.

Many urged Levinson's name for a Nobel Peace Prize following this accomplishment. Various universities gave him honorary degrees, and he was made a chevalier of the French Legion of Honor. Time magazine, in its article on its 1929 Man of the Year (neither Levinson nor Kellogg) wrote:

> *Undoubtedly there may be historians who will find the name of Frank Billings Kellogg brightest in 1929, for it was the year in which 57 nations signed the world-peace treaty with his name on it. But researchers and analysts could show that Mr. Kellogg did not originate the outlawing-war idea; that a comparatively obscure lay figure named Salmon Oliver Levinson, Chicago lawyer, was invited to the White House the day the signatures were affixed in recognition of certain conversations he had had years prior with Senator Borah of Idaho and others.*

Coolidge signs the Kellogg-Briand Pact into U.S. law.

WHAT GOOD DID IT DO

In the 19th century there was no compulsory adjudication of international disputes, no crime in warmaking, and states could claim title by conquest. The Kellogg-Briand Pact established the practice of not recognizing territorial claims gained through war, and its revival by another crusading lawyer during World War II (the Pact having been largely forgotten by then) created prosecutions of the crime of aggression — ironically so, in that the Pact had been created precisely in order to avoid creating a crime called aggression. Victors' justice is not full justice, but punishing leaders following World War II worked out a whole lot better than had punishing an entire nation after World War I. The moral and legal thinking advanced by the Pact also led to the creation of the United Nations and the International Criminal Court. The Kellogg-Briand Pact, by including both the United States and the Soviet Union, meant in some measure the first U.S. recognition of the Soviet Union's existence. In 1932, Secretary of State Henry Stimson wrote in *Foreign Affairs*:

> War between nations was renounced by the signatories of the Briand-Kellogg Pact. This means that it has become illegal throughout practically the entire world. It is no longer to be the source and subject of rights. It is no longer to be the principle around which the duties, the conduct, and the rights of nations revolve. It is an illegal thing. Hereafter when two nations engage in armed conflict either one or

both of them must be wrongdoers — violators of the general treaty. We no longer draw a circle about them and treat them with the punctilios of the duelist's code. Instead we denounce them as law breakers.

Vinson wrote of Stimson:

Shortly after he took office it began to appear that Russia and China would forget the solemn pledge of the Pact of Paris and go to war on the Manchurian border. This eventuality Stimson wished to avoid at all costs, as the ceremony proclaiming the pact to be in full and final effect was to take place July 24, 1929. It would be a tragedy for war to break out, as seemed quite likely, on or just before this date. . . . Seeking to call a halt to the threatened hostilities, he appealed to the Russians and to the Chinese to honor their treaty obligations. Immediate hostilities were avoided and the Pact was proclaimed in peace rather than in war.

Numerous nations had called Russia and China's attention to their obligations under the Kellogg-Briand Pact. When Russia eventually invaded anyway, the same point was urged, and peace was made with Russia withdrawing.

When, two years later, Japan invaded Manchuria, the United States declared that it would not recognize any agreement brought about by a violation of the Kellogg-Briand Pact, and the League of Nations voted to take the same position. This nonrecognition of the spoils of war was new and followed from the recategorization of war as a crime by the Outlawry movement and the Pact. The idea can be found in a 1919 plan proposed by Levinson for Senator Knox. Six years after the ratification of the Pact, Italy invaded Ethiopia. Next, Germany and the Soviet Union would invade Poland. World war would come again. The highest achievement of the peace movement was not nearly enough to counteract decades of dangerous policies. But the possibility of avoiding war had been, ever so briefly, demonstrated.

Frank Kellogg said in Oslo, Norway, when receiving the Nobel Prize for Peace in 1930:

> *It was not an ordinary treaty entered into by nations to serve as temporary advantage, like treaties of amity or alliance; it was a sacred promise between all nations and to all peoples of the world not to go to war for the settlement of their differences; to use a common phrase, to 'outlaw' war; to make it a crime against the law of nations so that any nations which violate it should be condemned by the public opinion of the world.*

> *I know there are those who believe that peace will not be attained until some super-tribunal is established to punish the violators of such treaties, but I believe in the end the abolition of war, the maintenance of world peace, the adjustment of international questions by pacific means will come through the force of public opinion, which controls nations and peoples — that public opinion which shapes our destinies and guides the progress of human affairs.*

The very next month after the Kellogg-Briand Pact had been signed in Paris, the League of Nations had passed the General Act for the Pacific Settlement of International Disputes, which has played its own role in advancing the development of public opinion and legal precedent. But this tradition developed as a countercurrent to the advancement of fascism and militarism through the depression of the 1930s. A new world court to rule on the crime of war was not created. Only measures acceptable to isolationism/exceptionalism, namely the Kellogg-Briand Pact and weapons increases, made it through the U.S. Senate. In 1931, Senator Borah remarked:

> *Much has been said, and will continue to be said, for the doctrine of force dies hard, about implementing the peace pact. It is said that we must put teeth into it — an apt word revealing again that theory of peace which is based upon tearing, maiming, destroying, murdering. Many have inquired of me: What is meant by implementing the peace pact? I will seek to make it plain. What they mean is to change the peace pact into a military pact. They would transform it into another peace scheme based upon force, and force is another name for war. By putting teeth into it, they mean an agreement to employ armies and navies wherever the fertile mind of some ambitious schemer can find an aggressor . . . I have no language to express my horror of this proposal to build peace treaties, or peace schemes, upon the doctrine of force.*

Shotwell's 1936 book, *On the Rim of the Abyss*, looked back in its preface at the creation of the League and of the

Kellogg-Briand Pact as both were already considered failures, particularly with the Italian invasion of Ethiopia. Shotwell argued that ending war would take generations, and that there were successes as well as failures to be learned from in what had been accomplished thus far.

Levinson died in 1941, as did mainstream thinking about the Outlawry of war.

I asked noted military historian William Blum how quickly the United States had itself violated the Kellogg-Briand Pact. He pointed to U.S. war making in Nicaragua between 1926 and 1933, the landing of U.S. forces in China in 1932, a U.S. Navy show of force in Cuba in 1933, and marines landing in China in 1934. In 1940, the United States obtained bases in Newfoundland, Bermuda, St. Lucia, the Bahamas, Jamaica, Antigua, Trinidad, and British Guiana. In 1941, the United States took control of Greenland and Iceland, and occupied Dutch Guiana, while also attacking German submarines and providing weapons to Britain and Russia.

Once the Second World War had begun, efforts were made to blame not militarism, fascism, and vindictive policies of the preceding decades, but efforts toward peace. Some claimed that the Kellogg-Briand Pact had lulled the allies to sleep while the axis had prepared for war. Quincy Wright, in the introduction to Stoner's book, argued against this idea: "The instrument served as a stimulus rather than a deterrent to more effective international organization." That certainly seems to have been the case. Additional efforts to create structures for peace accelerated after

August 1928. They were just not enough or not in time to prevent the worst event yet recorded in that day or this on the planet earth.

Stimson, as detailed in my book *War Is A Lie*, worked to provoke Japan, urged war on Germany, and developed the nuclear bomb, just as at an earlier time he had backed imperial control of Nicaragua and the Philippines where he had once served as Governor General. Yet, in the peace-hungry climate of 1928, Stimson supported Outlawry, and when World War II was underway, he would support Outlawry trials for the losing side.

WAR CRIMES TRIALS

Following World War II, a charge was needed through which German leaders could be held accountable for what the allies considered "the German problem," namely the aggressions of 1939, 1914, 1870, 1866, 1864, and others. The Kellogg-Briand Pact had been neglected and dismissed during the 1930s. Its revival for use in post-World War II criminal trials for Germans and Japanese was not the work of a popular movement, but it was the work of a lawyer in New York who pursued his idea with Levinsonian determination.

William Chanler's efforts to revive the Kellogg-Briand Pact are recounted in Jonathan A. Bush's *Columbia Law Review* article from December 2002 titled "'The Supreme International Crime' and Its Origins: The Lost Legislative History of the Crime of Aggressive War." Here's the context:

> *Very few of the wartime authors, even the lawyers, took that next step of calling for trials for an identifiable legal crime of planning, initiating, or waging aggressive war. There are obvious reasons why they did not. For one thing, aggressive war as a triable crime was essentially as lacking in precedent in 1943 as it had been in 1919, when it was rejected as being without precedent, unless one thought that the discredited Kellogg-Briand Pact had sufficiently changed the law. And because there was no explicit precedent criminalizing*

aggression, most authors concluded in formulaic manner that after victory there should be judicial punishment for those who had committed atrocities, and a harsh but not necessarily legal response to aggression, based on joint Allied decision. Those who only a few years before had hoped for more, putting their faith in a strong prohibition of aggression under Versailles and Kellogg-Briand, saw that those texts, and their vision, had manifestly failed, and presumably they were loathe to propose again the same failed solutions. In fact, some commentators now looked back ruefully and said they should have endorsed not peace or neutrality but aggressive intervention against Germany as early as 1934. In a telling sign of the mood, they did not call it humanitarian intervention, but aggression —aggression as virtue.

Yet, even those law professors whom Bush quotes arguing in the 1940s against prosecution of war making, or "aggressive war making," universally note that such prosecution would be morally sound, even if legally unsupported. These asides, noting the self-evident moral good of such a cause, would not have been made in previous centuries. Kellogg-Briand had indeed accomplished something invisible to but internalized by its analysts.

And then came Wall Street lawyer William Chamberlain Chanler (1895-1981), an associate of by-then Secretary of War Stimson's:

Chanler . . . joined the fray by submitting to Secretary Stimson a memorandum dated November 30, 1944 . . . .

Chanler wrote that the solution was to recognize that Kellogg-Briand and related instruments had determined that aggressive wars — wars not fought in self-defense — were illegal. If they were, then it followed, for example, that persons carrying guns and committing killings in Poland or Czechoslovakia were not privileged combatants, as they would be if they were lawful fighters in a lawful war under the traditional laws and customs of war. They were, instead, legally unprivileged fighters — men using violence without legal justification or excuse, men whom the law terms ordinary criminals — committing violations of Polish or Czech domestic criminal law.

Thus did Chanler present the crime of aggression as a doorway to prosecuting numerous secondary war crimes. He made his case in letters to various law professors involved in the planning of possible post-war trials. In one, he wrote,

I feel we are in great danger of writing off the Kellogg Pact, which, after all, not only embodies traditional U.S. policy regarding war, but was adopted largely at our instigation, as a mere scrap of paper. I do not think that we as Americans should support such a possibility. I feel on the contrary that it is quite possible to give real meaning to the pact, and that we should use every effort to do so.

And in another he wrote,

To my mind, your arguments are completely unpersuasive,

and you have not yet answered the question which I now ask
for the fifth time: 'what does the Kellogg Pact mean?' I am
coming to the conclusion that you intend to insist until your
dying breath that it was a mere scrap of paper. To take such
a position, I consider, (to use your own language), a 'distinct
disservice to the U.S. and to the cause of future world peace'
— only I would use stronger language.

Failing to win over legal academe to his cause, Chanler targeted someone else with his argument: President Franklin Delano Roosevelt.

Chanler had worked in the Pentagon (and perhaps Italy
as well) alongside Colonel John Boettiger, publisher of the
Seattle Post-Intelligencer *and, more importantly, President*
Roosevelt's son-in-law, who from time to time made family
visits to the President. Chanler wrote a short (lost) cover
note to his languishing November 30 memorandum,
explaining it for Boettiger's (and the President's) benefit.
Boettiger took the idea to Hyde Park. Perhaps Boettiger had
his own reasons for liking the idea, for he too was involved
in planning for postwar Germany, albeit apparently not
on war crimes matters. On January 3, 1945, came a short
memo from the President indicating his approval of various
departmental war crimes proposals that had been presented
to him, along with the President's initials on Chanler's
(lost) cover note. To the surprise of almost everyone except
Chanler, the last lines of the president's memo said that 'the
charges should include an indictment for waging aggressive

warfare, in violation of the Kellogg Pact. Perhaps these and other charges might be joined in a conspiracy indictment.'

And, lo and behold, suddenly a number of bureaucrats came to believe that Chanler's idea had a really solid basis in the law after all. Nazi leaders were charged with atrocities but also with the making of war itself. Those leaders included government officials and complicit industrialists. Among the officials were diplomats who had threatened war and never launched it against nations that had preemptively surrendered. Twenty-two defendants were charged with Conspiracy to Commit Crimes Against Peace, and eight of them were convicted. Some were very likely acquitted in part because German industry was viewed in Washington, as these trials dragged on and on, just as it had been viewed on Wall Street prior to the war, namely as a force for good in opposition to the Soviet danger.

The International Military Tribunal at Nuremberg described the launching of war as "not only an international crime; it is the supreme international crime, differing only from other war crimes in that it contains within itself the accumulated evil of the whole." The Tokyo Tribunal, as well, drew on and referenced the Kellogg-Briand Pact.

The Chief Prosecutor at Nuremberg, U.S. Supreme Court Justice Robert H. Jackson, said in his opening statement,

The common sense of mankind demands that law shall not stop with the punishment of petty crimes by little people. It

must also reach men who possess themselves of great power and make deliberate and concerted use of it to set in motion evils which leave no home in the world untouched. The Charter of this Tribunal evidences a faith that the law is not only to govern the conduct of little men, but that even rulers are, as Lord Chief Justice Coke put it to King James, 'under ... the law.' And let me make clear that while this law is first applied against German aggressors, the law includes, and if it is to serve a useful purpose it must condemn aggression by any other nations, including those which sit here now in judgment.

Cornel West at a nonviolent occupation
of Wall Street in New York in 2011.

PURSUING PEACE

In September 2011, I gave a lecture at a college in which I summarized the ideas in this book. Before I began, I asked the students and professors to raise their hands if they believed war was illegal or if they had ever heard of the Kellogg-Briand Pact. About 2 or 3 percent of the people in a large ballroom raised their hands. That didn't shock me. But I also asked if they thought war *should* be illegal, and the response was no more than 5 percent. That never fails to disturb me.

Nobody's ever read the Kellogg-Briand Pact or the U.N. Charter. Fine. O.K. Nobody's ever read anything. But if I'd asked whether slavery or rape should be illegal, every hand would have gone up. As recently as 2000, I could have asked whether torture should be illegal, and every hand would have gone up. If I'd asked about genocide, every hand would have been in the air. Why not war?

Daniel Jonah Goldhagen's 2009 book, *Worse Than War: Genocide, Eliminationism, and the Ongoing Assault on Humanity,* works from the premise that a movement to outlaw war exists, but that it is misguided in that a far worse crime is mass murder. I would like such a movement to exist, but I don't see the value Goldhagen does in teasing apart war and mass murder and determining which deaths belong in which category. In my view, war is mass murder. Killing your own people is no worse, and no better, than killing another nation's people. The propaganda that drives wars and genocides is very similar. Goldhagen's analysis of what motivates mass murderers is very similar to what motivates warriors. Why try to separate them? And which category would you squeeze something like a CIA drone war into? Is it a war or a mass murder? What about melting the skin off children with white phosphorous in Fallujah, Iraq? Is that mass murder or war?

Hitler killed millions of Germans, epitomizing evil. But the allies killed as many or more Germans, Germans ordered into battle by Hitler or Germans in the wrong place when the bombs fell and the fires raged. Consider the current U.S. attitude that urges the blaming of policy makers but "supporting" of troops. Now apply it to the troops on all sides of all wars. They're all obeying orders made by policy makers. If troops are victims, they are a very large category of victims, as are the civilians who are the vast majority of the victims in what Goldhagen calls "legitimate war." The United States has no Department of Mass Murder but does have a Department of War (renamed the Department of Defense in 1947) which, together with other security spending, devours 65 percent of federal discretionary funds. Goldhagen sees no problem here, and thereby misses the surest way to make mass murder unacceptable: make war unacceptable. If wars could not be justified, then neither could mass murders. And our society is going to great lengths to see that the institution of war is justified.

Goldhagen considers the 2003 Iraq War "just," as he does the 2001 Afghanistan War and World War II. Palestinians only ever enter his worldview as murderers, never as victims. He claims that al Qaeda committed genocide on September 11, 2001, but that the

2003 Iraq War (still going on as I write) is not genocide. So there's a distinction that has nothing to do with the scale of the killing. At issue is the motivation behind the killing, or — less charitably — the question of whether the killing is in harmony with the interests of the U.S. government or not.

What's needed is not less effort to end genocide. We need much greater focus and energy there. But we also need a revival of the Outlawry of war, along with its analysis of what war amounts to. A more faithful revival of Outlawry than what was managed after World War II might serve us very well. The Kellogg-Briand Pact, which has never been repealed, makes a stronger case against wars like Afghanistan and Iraq than does the U.N. Charter. To comply with Kellogg-Briand, wars need not be defensive or U.N.-authorized. Rather, wars need to simply not exist.

Outlawry also removes a major reason why young men and women join the military — namely to make war as a means to achieving peace. If there is no way to peace other than peace, if war cannot have a noble cause, if war has been — as it formally has been — renounced as an instrument of policy, then idealistic militarism goes away from recruiting offices, and the propaganda of humanitarian war suffers as well.

And why not revive Outlawry by reviving its accomplishment, the Kellogg-Briand Pact? The Pact has never been repealed, and as Denys P. Myers noted in his 1929 book, *Origin and Conclusion of the Paris Pact*, "The treaty contains no provision for its abrogation or for the withdrawal of any party. Its engagements must, therefore, be regarded as a permanent contract, without time limit among and between the contracting parties."

If a case were brought to court in the United States under the Kellogg-Briand Pact today, it would face the argument that no criminal punishment and no private cause of action were created by the pact. It would face claims of "state secrets" that prevent wars being discussed. It would face the "political question" argument that such decisions do not belong to the judiciary branch at all. And if such a case were brought against the United States in a foreign or international court, it would face the "Shut up, he explained" argument from Washington through all of our government's ways of exerting influence. But all such arguments, domestically or abroad, can be removed through a cultural shift. Laws are not just written words. They are, for better or worse, what people choose to say they are. If the Fourth Amendment to the U.S. Constitution can be interpreted to allow the U.S. government to read my emails and listen to my phone calls without a warrant, then surely the Kellogg Briand Pact can again be interpreted to say exactly what it appears to say.

In his 1943 forward to *S.O. Levinson and the Pact of Paris*, John Dewey argued that the failure to prevent World War II emphasized "our need to recover and strengthen Levinson's faith that the great mass of men and women would welcome an era in which the war system has no standing and his faith in the possibility of social means by which to secure this end."

If we are to succeed in that effort, we may benefit from studying the activism that originally promoted Outlawry. The movement of the 1920s was principled, non-partisan, trans-ideological, and unrelenting. More internationalist and more principled anti-imperialist or disarmament proposals, and the proposal to create a public referendum power to block wars, all helped to make Outlawry mainstream by comparison, just as third-party pressure improved the Republicans and Democrats. The campaign was built over a period of years through both education and the cultivation of powerful supporters. It was not overly distracted by elections. Its analysis included cold cost-benefit calculations, but front and center was always the morality of the cause of ending war. This campaign worked internationally, nationally, and locally. And its members did not believe victory would come in their lifetimes. But neither were they so focused on themselves as to imagine that this somehow made eventual victory impossible. They were convinced, as I am, that if Outlawry does not win, humanity will lose.

A couple of points deserve further emphasis. First, the campaign to pass the Kellogg-Briand Pact was driven by an uncomfortably large coalition. People who did not trust or generally agree with each other pursued this together, because on this they were in agreement. Half the peace movement, the Outlawrist half, got exactly what it wanted, or at least a step in the exact direction it wanted to move in. The other half, the pro-League half, got perhaps its second choice, or at least something it very much favored, even though its top desire was in a different direction.

Second, activist groups did not invert the representational process in the manner that is now common. They took a popular demand to the government. They did not go to government officials of one party or the other and ask, "What should we tell our members to ask you to do?" That inversion of representative government has become the norm, leading to public disillusionment with activist groups, labor unions, and other organizations that purport to lobby public servants while actually treating us as the servants of the public servants. That mindset is also internalized by many U.S. residents who believe their duty is to a party or a politician, rather than the politicians' duty being to majority opinion.

One of the most glaring questions that arise in comparing peace activism of the 1920s and the 2000s is this: why did rich people support peace back then? One answer is that the culture as a whole was different. Churches backed peace. Academics backed peace. Support for peace was not unique to robber barons. Peace was something to be imposed on backward Europeans. Peace was American, patriotic, nationalistic, and a continuation or fulfillment of the glory of the Great War. Peace did not require opposing any particular actual war. It did not require opposing the central agenda of the U.S. government. It did not require going up against the military industrial complex, which did not yet exist. Farmers had more pull than weapons makers. The communications system was not in the hands of an international corporate cartel with profit interests in wars. Bribery of elected officials was considered criminal. Nowadays, corruption is king, and peace is anti-American.

My local newspaper reported in September 2011 on a local school board member's objection to a resolution in support of events celebrating the International Day of Peace. "I'm all in favor of peace and non-violence," this gentleman said, "but, for instance . . . to the extent that any of the events are really sort of anti-war events, I'm not necessarily comfortable with supporting that." This is typical. People favor "peace on earth" while considering it vaguely treasonous to oppose actual wars. This is a major handicap for peace efforts in an age of perpetual war making.

That can be changed, but it will take work. It will require slowly building sustainable structural support for a peace movement. Such a movement could also learn from the Twenties that open advocacy of unlikely causes works much better than self-censorship. Of the many creative proposals for peace that gained popularity during the 1920s, one of the most intriguing is the idea of requiring a public referendum before launching any war.

William Jennings Bryan in 1916 urged that a public referendum be required before going to war. Col. George Harvey proposed a war referendum to Senator Warren Harding in 1920. Thomas Hall Shastid's 1927 book, *Give the People Their Own War Power*, makes the case for a referendum power perhaps as well as any other text. Senator Borah favored the idea in 1927: "No war should be begun, except in absolute defense, until the question has been submitted to those who are to do the fighting," he said. Of course, Borah favored banning all wars not fought in absolute defense and did so with the Kellogg-Briand Pact. He did not attempt to create a referendum power.

The case for a referendum, like the case for outlawing war, was and is based on the understanding that most people do not want war. Conscription is required to get people to go to war, Shastid argued, because they do not want it. Only a small number of powerful people in any country ever want war, he claimed, and only four or five major countries determine whether wars engulf the world. A referendum power is also compatible with continued self-defense to an extent that Outlawry may not obviously be. That is to say, a nation could continue dumping its funds into massive weapons production, while creating a requirement to hold a referendum before going to war. And a war of actual self-defense could be expected to be approved by a referendum. Shastid complained, on the other hand, that ministers and churches were not supporting the referendum demand. If church leaders found submitting war decisions to a public vote overly democratic in 1927, they might hold the same view today; that might be one hurdle to be overcome.

The story of the war referendum could fill another book. Ben Manski, in a paper on my warisacrime.org website called "The Struggle to Put Ballots Before Bullets," traces the idea to Immanuel Kant and the Marquis de Condorcet, through an 1809 proposal by the Reverend John Foster in Boston, Mass. The idea was brought to Congress during World War I by Representative Richard Bartholdt, a Republican from New York, and Senator La Follette of Wisconsin. The movement reached its peak in 1938 when the Ludlow Amendment proposing a Constitutional Amendment appeared likely to pass through Congress, and an American Institute for Public Opinion survey found that 73 percent of Americans favored it. President Franklin Roosevelt wrote to the Speaker of the House asking that it be defeated, and it was, by a vote of 209-188. Roosevelt twisted the necessary arms to defeat the amendment. The same idea hasn't even been introduced as legislation since 1971, but perhaps it should be.

Other proposals shaping the peace movement of the 1920s focused on disarmament, including unilateral disarmament. Proposals of later decades, the 1950s and 1960s, have promoted conversion from military to nonmilitary industries. A successful peace movement will pursue such agendas.

Progress toward peace and social justice has always lost ground during wars and been obliged to make it up in between them. So, our first step must be ending current wars and arriving at an interlude of peace at least in the sense of a pause during which everybody is busy reloading.

We should then draw on the wisdom of Outlawry and disentangle ourselves from alliances that require us to go to war, including the North Atlantic Treaty Organization (NATO).

As was done after World War I, we must learn and teach the horrors and financial costs of our wars, as well as the costs to the natural environment, civil liberties, and every other area. We must deepen public understanding that nobody wins a war any more than anybody wins a hurricane. We must build awareness of how much higher the stakes have grown, now that we risk total destruction through nuclear weapons or environmental degradation.

We must stop worrying about whom to elect and start learning how to pressure those who are in office.

We must stop getting discouraged. We must also stop getting optimistic. Instead we need to learn to enjoy working for the moral good for its own sake, not ours. "It is not likely that I shall live to see the war making power placed in the hands of the people, even in one single country," wrote Shastid, "Nevertheless it is something to have worked for the right."

We should learn to support multiple strategies (Outlawry, referendum power, disarmament, etc.) without framing each as the rival or enemy of the others. Here are some:

- Cut a half a trillion dollars out of the $1.2 trillion national security budget, putting half of it into tax cuts for non-billionaires, and half of it into useful spending on green energy, education, retraining for displaced military-industrial workers, etc.
- Bring the National Guard home and de-federalize it.
- Ban the redeployment of personnel currently suffering PTSD.
- Ban no-bid uncompeted military contracts.
- Restore constitutional war powers to the Congress.
- Create a requirement for a public referendum prior to launching any war.
- Close the foreign bases.
- Ban weapons from space.

- Ban extra-legal prisons.
- Ban kangaroo military courts outside of our ordinary court system.
- Restore habeas corpus.
- Ban the use of mercenaries.
- Limit military spending to no more than twice that of the next highest spending nation on earth.
- Ban secret budgets, secret agencies, and secret operations.
- Ban the launching of drone strikes into foreign nations.
- Forbid the transfer of students' information to military recruiters without their permission.
- Comply with the Kellogg-Briand Pact.
- Reform or replace the United Nations.
- Join the International Criminal Court and make it independent of the United Nations.
- Disarm.

We should stop appealing purely to people's selfishness with arguments about financial costs or U.S. casualties and appeal also to their goodness and decency.

We should remember the Kellogg-Briand Pact and create a holiday for that purpose on August 27th.

We should revive Outlawry, but stop imagining that we have to reinvent the wheel. One of General Douglas MacArthur's last speeches sounds as if he had invented the notion of Outlawry, and as if it wasn't already on the books. This speech is still worth reading:

The great question is: Can global war now be outlawed from the world? If so, it would mark the greatest advance in civilization since the Sermon on the Mount. It would lift at one stroke the darkest shadow which has engulfed mankind from the beginning. It would not only remove fear and bring security — it would not only create new moral and spiritual values — it would produce an economic wave of prosperity that would raise the world's standard of living beyond anything ever dreamed of by man. The hundreds of billions of dollars now spent in mutual preparedness [for war] could conceivably abolish poverty from the face of the earth. It would accomplish even more than this; it would at one stroke reduce the international tensions that seem to be insurmountable now, to matters of more probable solution. . . . Many will tell you with mockery and ridicule that the abolition of war can be only a dream — that it is but the vague imagining of a visionary. But we must go on or we will go under. And the great criticism that can be made is that the world lacks a plan that will enable us to go on. We have suffered the blood and the sweat and the tears. Now we seek the way and the truth and the light. We are in a new era. The old methods and solutions for this vital problem no longer suffice. We must have new thoughts, new ideas, new concepts. . . . We must have sufficient imagination and courage to translate this universal wish for peace — which is rapidly becoming a universal necessity — into actuality.

On September 23, 2011, the Chairman of the Joint Chiefs of

Staff Michael Mullen blamed Pakistan for "choosing to use violent extremism as an instrument of policy." Almost certainly very few if any readers or viewers of that comment heard an echo in it. We long ago led the world in renouncing as an instrument of policy something far worse than violent extremism, something to which we now devote 65 percent of our national discretionary budget, something which — in the end — is good for absolutely nothing: war.

> *"Just one step toward peace means a great success if one is determined to take another step the next day."*
> — *Aristide Briand.*

Acknowledgements

Linda Swanson did research, editing, and locating of photographs. The University of Virginia Library and the HoosOnline website were very useful. Bruce Levine provided editing suggestions that made the book more readable. Ben Manski sent helpful suggestions, including encouragement to discuss the Socialist and Progressive Parties. Ben Davis directed me toward the story of William Chanler's revival of the Kellogg-Briand Pact in the 1940s. Paul Chappell pointed me toward the Douglas MacArthur quotation at the end of the book. William Blum steered me toward good information on the International Criminal Court. Bob Fertik suggested ideas for promoting and then helped to promote this book. The progressive online groups rootsaction.org and democrats.com provided a flexible schedule and the means to write this book while otherwise employed. The front cover photo is by Norbert Nagel of Mörfelden-Walldorf, Germany. The photo of Salmon Levinson was taken by Linda Swanson; it is a photo of a sketch found at the Library of Congress, New York World-Telegram & Sun Collection.

A note on publishing: It may soon seem superfluous to mention this, but in 2011 there are still people who believe a book should be published by a publisher. I turned publishers away in order to publish this myself. I kept complete editorial control. I laid the book out and designed it on my laptop. I published it when I wanted to, rather than a year later. And of the little bit of money the book generates, I will not be giving the bulk of it to someone who didn't write the book. If the book generates a significant amount of money, I will be giving it to the peace movement — just like Carnegie, only without the exploitation and union busting.

David Swanson arrested at the White House opposing wars.

David Swanson, at right, leads a march in 2011.

About the Author

David Swanson's previous books are *War Is A Lie* and *Daybreak: Undoing the Imperial Presidency and Forming a More Perfect Union*. He blogs at davidswanson.org and warisacrime.org and works for the online activist organizations rootsaction.org and democrats.com. Swanson holds a master's degree in philosophy from the University of Virginia. He has worked as a newspaper reporter and as a communications director, with jobs including press secretary for Dennis Kucinich's 2004 presidential campaign, media coordinator for the International Labor Communications Association, and three years as communications coordinator for ACORN, the Association of Community Organizations for Reform Now.

CPSIA information can be obtained at www.ICGtesting.com
Printed in the USA
LVOW031924191011

251294LV00006B/1/P